50 *hikes* in
Eastern Pennsylvania

50 hikes
in
Eastern Pennsylvania

From the Mason-Dixon Line
to the Poconos and North Mountain

Third Edition

TOM THWAITES

Backcountry Publications
Woodstock, Vermont

An Invitation to the Reader

Over time trails can be rerouted and signs and landmarks altered. If you nd that changes have occurred on the routes described in this book, please let us know so that corrections may be made in future editions. The author and publisher also welcome other comments and suggestions. Address all correspondence to:

Editor, *50 Hikes*™ Series
Backcountry Publications
PO Box 748
Woodstock, VT 05091

Library of Congress Cataloging-in-Publication Data

Thwaites, Tom.
Fifty hikes in eastern Pennsylvania : from the Mason-Dixon line to the Poconos and North Mountain / Tom Thwaites. — 3rd ed.
    p. cm.
Includes index.
ISBN 0-88150-372-X
    1. Hiking—Pennsylvania—Guidebooks. 2. Backpacking—Pennsylvania—Guidebooks. 3. Trails—Pennsylvania—Guidebooks. 4. Pennsylvania—Guidebooks. I. Title. IV.
GV199.42.P4T485   1997
795.51'09748—dc21
                                                        96-48310
                                                        CIP

Published by Backcountry Publications
An imprint of The Countryman Press
PO Box 748
Woodstock, VT 05091

Distributed by
W.W. Norton & Co., Inc.
500 Fifth Avenue
New York, NY 10110

Series design by Glenn Suokko
Trail overlays by Richard Widhu
Cover photograph and interior photographs by Tom Thwaites
Printed in the United States of America

10 9 8 7 6 5 4 3 2 1

DEDICATION

To Emily and Jeremy Batt, the next generation of hikers

ACKNOWLEDGMENTS

Many of the hikes in this book were suggested by employees of the Pennsylvania Bureau of State Parks, the National Park Service, the Pennsylvania Bureau of Forestry, and members of the Keystone Trails Association.

I thank Oreste Unti, Tom Davidowski, John Seville, Ron Gray, James Becker, James Flandreau, Mike Cosgrove, Erik Williams, Larry Pittis, Joe and Lorraine Healey, Matt Marcinek, Tom Scully, Mark Arbogast, Steve McGuire, Karen Lutz, and many others whose names I didn't get or forgot to write down. I am particularly grateful to my wife, Barbara, who served as hiking companion, driver, typist, and editor.

50 Hikes at a Glance

Location

South Mountain	1. Caledonia	Chambersburg
	2. Pole Steeple	South Mountain
	3. Kings Gap	South Mountain
	4. Gifford Pinchot	York
	5. Gettysburg	Gettysburg
	6. Sunset Rocks	South Mountain
	7. Cumberland Valley	Carlisle
	8. Peters Mountain	Harrisburg
	9. Stone Tower	Saint Anthony's
	10. Rausch Gap	Saint Anthony's
Philadelphia and Vicinity	11. Jacobsburg	Easton
	12. High Rocks	Easton
	13. Middle Creek	Reading
	14. Susquehannock	Lancaster
	15. Nolde Forest	Reading
	16. Ridley Creek	Media
	17. Skippack Creek	Norristown
	18. Wissahickon Gorge	Philadelphia
	19. Valley Forge	Norristown
	20. Holtwood	Lancaster
	21. Tyler State Park	Philadelphia
	22. Mill Creek	Reading
	23. The Pinnacle	Hamburg
	24. Wilderness Trail	Media
	25. Delaware Canal	Easton
	26. French Creek	Reading
	27. Blue Marsh Lake	Reading

Distance (in kilometers)	Rise (in meters)	View	Good for kids	Camping nearby	X-C skiing	Notes
4.7	175		✓	✓		
8.7	232	✓		✓		
10.1	340	✓	✓			
11.1	80		✓	✓		
13.0	140	✓	✓			view from Little Round Top
13.3	323	✓		✓		
16.5	135					
7.6	315	✓				
12.1	395					
15.8	215				✓	ski on S&SRR grade
4.0	65	✓	✓		✓	
4.3	60	✓	✓			railings at clifftop
5.3	130	✓	✓			
5.6	220	✓	✓			
5.8	146		✓			
6.9	150		✓			
7.5	100		✓			
7.6	140		✓			
7.8	85		✓			
8.1	250	✓	✓			
8.7	110		✓			
10.9	320			✓		
14.0	315	✓		✓		camping at Blue Rocks campground
14.1	245		✓			hike can be truncated; $3 admission
17.3	15					
18.5	353		✓			
22.5	385					

50 Hikes at a Glance

		Location
The Poconos	28. Hawk Falls	Poconos
	29. Skyline Trail	Poconos
	30. Blooming Grove	Poconos
	31. Bradys Lake	Poconos
	32. Mount Minsi	Stroudsburg
	33. Dingmans Falls	Poconos
	34. Lakeside Trail	Poconos
	35. Gouldsboro	Poconos
	36. Choke Creek	Poconos
	37. Big Pocono	Stroudsburg
	38. Boulder Field	Poconos
	39. Pennel Run	Poconos
	40. Bruce Lake	Poconos
	41. Big Bear Swamp	Poconos
	42. Promised Land	Poconos
	43. Thunder Swamp	Poconos
	44. Painter Creek	Poconos
	45. Fourth Run	Poconos
North Mountain	46. Frances Slocum	Wilkes-Barre
	47. Joe Gmiter	Wilkes-Barre
	48. Ricketts Glen	North Mountain
	49. Mount Pisgah	Towanda
	50. Cherry Run	North Mountain

Distance (in kilometers)	Rise (in meters)	View	Good for kids	Camping nearby	X-C skiing	Notes
4.8	135		✓	✓		carry kids across stream
7.8	215	✓	✓	✓	✓	carry kids across stream
7.9	90		✓		✓	
7.9	45		✓		✓	
7.9	310	✓				
8.0	160			✓		camp at Dingmans campground
8.3	25		✓	✓	✓	
9.1	91		✓	✓	✓	camp at Tobyhanna State Park
10.0	90		✓			
11.1	295	✓				
11.3	170		✓	✓		
11.4	220					
11.8	98		✓	✓	✓	camp at Promised Land State Park
14.2	220			✓		
14.2	110			✓		
15.1	250					
15.6	280	✓				
20.0	285			✓	✓	ski west of PA 534
5.3	67		✓	✓		
7.2	320					
10.7	315			✓		
11.0	365	✓				ski elsewhere in park
21.5	225			✓		

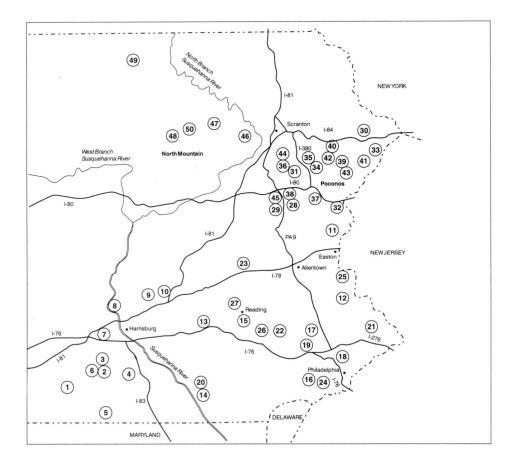

Contents

NORTH MOUNTAIN

INDEX

INTRODUCTION

Hiking is a particular delight to me. Every season there are new things to discover, even on the same old trail. Wildflowers of spring give way to the soft green velvet beauty of summer, which in turn gives way to the color riot of autumn, followed by the snows of winter, with their many animal tracks.

All of us return to the roots of our species when we walk. Our ancestors were bipedal long before they were human. They walked out of the jungle into the veldt and then all over the earth. As an anthropologist would say, bipedalism (walking on two feet) preceded encephalization (swelling of the brain). Our cousins who persisted in walking on their knuckles are still in the Gombe Preserve.

Nessmuck wrote: "We do not go to the woods to rough it, we go to smooth it. We get it rough enough in town." "Nessmuck" is the pen name of George Washington Sears (1821–90), Pennsylvania's pioneer conservationist and outdoor writer.

"Climb the mountains and get their good tidings. Nature's peace will flow into you, and the storms their energy, while cares drop off like autumn leaves," is the way John Muir put it.

According to Thomas Jefferson, "Walking is the best possible exercise. Habituate yourself to walk very far. The Europeans value themselves on having subdued the horse to the uses of man: but I doubt whether we have not lost more than we have gained, by the use of this animal."

And as Aldo Leopold said, "Never did we plan the morrow, for we had learned that in the wilderness some new and irresistible distraction is sure to turn up each day before breakfast."

Hiking in eastern Pennsylvania—despite our region's proximity to the cities along the coast—has much to offer. North Mountain is still wild and remote; the Poconos shelter the most secure portion of the state's bear population; the famous Appalachian Trail follows South and Blue Mountains across Pennsylvania. Saint Anthony's Wilderness, just 20 kilometers north of Harrisburg, is the second-largest wild area in the state. Although the state forests are smaller than average, there are many state parks and game lands— some quite large—as well as lands of some public utilities open to the public. A national recreation area and two national historic parks round out the roster. Public lands are limited in extent in eastern Pennsylvania, but well developed with trails.

Trails may traverse woodlands or follow old canals and roads, but many are multiuse, with bicycle and horse as well as foot traffic. On multiuse trails you must pay attention to the rights-of-way of the different trail users. Since horses are easily startled and may throw their riders (sometimes with fatal results), both hikers and bicyclists should give way to horses. Bikers should in turn give way to hikers.

While some trails are heavily used, on others you can still find solitude and a sense of remoteness. There are views, waterfalls, canals, streams, a Civil War battlefield, ghost towns, water gaps, and old railroad grades, as well as quiet paths through the woods and through the largest city park in the world.

GEOGRAPHY

Eastern Pennsylvania contains all the geographic provinces of the state, save one (the Lake Erie Lowlands). These include the Allegheny Plateau and the Ridge and Valley Province. Then, moving from Blue Mountain at the edge of the Ridge and Valley region toward Philadelphia, come the Great Valley; South Mountain and the Reading Prong; the Triassic Lowlands; the Piedmont; and the Coastal Plain.

The Pocono "Mountains" are a southern extension of the Allegheny Plateau, which consists of broad uplands cut by deep, narrow river valleys. The Ridge and Valley Province is made up of wide valleys separated by sharp, narrow ridges. The Allegheny Front forms the boundary between these two regions.

All the other regions lie in the lower right-hand corner of the state. The Great Valley extends from Georgia to New York State; in Pennsylvania it is formed of Cambrian and Ordovician rocks. South Mountain and the Reading Prong are made of Precambrian rocks. The Reading Prong is famous for its radon gas. The Triassic Lowlands were formed when the ancient supercontinent of Pangaea started to break apart about 200 million years ago. The Piedmont is made of a complex of metamorphic rocks of Paleozoic and Precambrian age. The Coastal Plain is of Cretaceous age and cuts across Philadelphia. Look in Van Diver's *Roadside Geology of Pennsylvania* for a map of these different regions.

A large part of eastern Pennsylvania was glaciated during the most recent, or Wisconsin, Ice Age. The limit of ice advance runs northwest from the Delaware Water Gap, passing through Hickory Run State Park and south of Ricketts Glen State Park. The glacier left scratches on the polished bedrock and great quantities of rocks and silt called glacial till. This debris filled preglacial valleys and forced streams to cut new valleys, with cascades and waterfalls. The glacier also left lakes and swamps—lots of swamps.

SAFETY IN THE WOODS

Once you've parked your car and put a few strong trees between you and the nearest road, the chances of your being injured or killed have dropped by an order of magnitude. Compared with our highways and roads, the woods are relatively safe.

Nevertheless, natural areas may contain hazards not otherwise encountered. Wild animals are seldom a problem. Bears are hunted every year; they know where you are and will ordinarily keep out of your way (if people haven't fed them). Count yourself fortunate if you catch even a glimpse of one. Instead, look for signs of bears. Bears protest your use of the trails by leaving piles of scat in the pathway;

still, they find using trails easier than crashing through the brush, so they do so. Look for footprints in wet places. They are remarkably human-looking, but wider. You can see all five toes. Look for claw marks at the ends of the toes. (Bears never cut their nails.) Male bears also make scratch marks on trees, particularly evergreens, by clawing off the bark. Watch for large rocks that have been turned over to get at ants underneath, or rotten logs that have been pulled apart for grubs.

Instead of bears, beware the cute little raccoon. Up to 75 percent of raccoons may be rabid, so avoid them all.

Native Americans said of Pennsylvania's animals, "When the pine needle falls from the tree the eagle sees it before it hits the ground, the deer hears the tiny thud, and the bear smells the puff of resin."

What about snakes? There may still be some specimens of timber rattlesnake and copperhead in eastern Pennsylvania. For too many years, though, people have believed that snakes were evil and had to be destroyed. If a snake had a buzzer at one end, then it was a rattlesnake and had to be killed. If it didn't, then it was a copperhead and had to be killed. Snakes have had a hard life in Pennsylvania. Of the 17 or more species of snake in the East, only two are poisonous, the timber rattlesnake and the copperhead. But don't pick up any snake: Most snakebites are on the hands or arms rather than the ankles or legs.

Snakes are the easiest wildlife to photograph since they may not flee at your approach. Rattlesnakes and copperheads are your friends, because they live on mice and small rodents. Deer ticks, which carry Lyme disease, spend more time on deer mice than they do on deer. Small rodents eat tree seeds and seedlings; overabundant rodents make it more difficult for the forest to regenerate. As John Muir said, "When we tug at a single thing in nature we find it attached to the rest of the world."

The real threats to your health are microscopic, such as *Giardia* and Lyme disease, or inanimate, such as cold and lightning.

Even the clearest stream or spring must be considered contaminated with *Giardia lamblia* and other harmful bacteria. The *Giardia* organism causes persistent diarrhea. On day hikes you can avoid contaminated water supplies by filling your canteen at home or from some other tested source. For longer trips you will have to purify your drinking water. The easiest way to do so in the field is with a submicron filter. A limitation of such filters is that you must use the cleanest water available or risk clogging the filter while filling a single canteen.

A lighter-weight and cheaper alternative for the patient is to add iodine tablets or drops and wait 20 minutes. A serious limitation is that the water must be at least 20 degrees C (68 degrees F) in order to kill *Giardia* cysts. Many find the iodine taste objectionable, but it can be obscured by adding flavoring to the drinking water. Some submicron filters incorporate an iodine stage. Boiling water to purify it (except in cooking) is recommended only by those who haven't tried it.

Lyme disease is an infection caused by a bacterium that can be transmitted by the bite of some species of ticks. In the eastern United States the *Ixodes*, or deer tick, is the culprit. Deer ticks are smaller than the common dog tick, which does not transmit Lyme disease. The nymph stage, which is responsible for most cases, is smaller than the period at the end of this sentence. The larger adult stage can be seen and removed before it can bite, but you're very unlikely to see the nymph stage. Nor will you feel the bite. Still, if you do discover a tick attached to you, remove it promptly with fine-point tweezers. Grab the tick where the mouthparts enter the skin, and pull gently and repeatedly until the tick lets go by withdrawing its mouthparts. Save the tick in a bottle of alcohol and call your local or state board of health to have it identified.

Ticks are most active in spring and summer—just when you want to go hiking. The conventional wisdom is to wear light-colored (to help you see ticks) long pants and to tuck the pants into your socks, but in warm weather this means you would be courting heat exhaustion instead. Let's face it: In spring, summer, and well into fall, you are going to wear shorts on the trail. What can you do to protect yourself? Spray 20 to 30 percent DEET on your socks and bare legs. (Permanone will keep ticks off your clothes and boots but should *not* be applied directly to your skin.) Keep to the middle of the trail; avoid wading through tall grass, brush, or ferns. Don't sit or lie on the ground. As soon as you get home, take a shower to sluice off any unattached ticks.

Blood tests for Lyme disease are still unreliable, so you must be aware of the symptoms and watch out for them. The first symptom is likely to be a slowly expanding red rash that may be centered at the site of the tick bite. The rash may appear from 1 to 4 weeks after the bite. There may be multiple rashes scattered around on parts of your body that are difficult to inspect, such as on your back, under your arms, and behind your knees.

The second symptoms of early Lyme disease are flulike and may include slight fever; headache; swollen glands; fatigue; and stiffness in the joints, neck, and jaw—but no cough or drippy nose. Lyme disease can be treated with antibiotics, and the sooner the better. Untreated Lyme disease can progress to more serious stages involving the joints, heart, and central nervous system, although it is rarely fatal. A vaccine for Lyme disease is undergoing clinical trials but is not yet available. (Considering the numbers of people at risk, there has been precious little research done on this disease.) If you think you may have been exposed, call the American Lyme Disease Foundation at 1-800-876-LYME for the name of a physician in your area who specializes in treating Lyme disease.

For 6 months of the year, whenever the temperature drops below 10 degrees C (50 degrees F), hypothermia stalks the unwary in Penn's Woods. You can forestall it by eating right (don't skip breakfast!), dressing right, and staying dry. Dress in layers so that if you get too hot, you can shed a layer and put it in your pack. (You can get just as wet from your own perspiration as you can from rain or falling into a stream.) Then when you start to feel cold, you can put the layer back on. Don't wait for shivering to start. With hypothermia, your judgment is the first thing to go.

Avoid tall trees and open places during thunderstorms. Along the trail, look for evidence of lightning strikes. A recent strike will appear as a light stripe on the tree and as a long strip of bark, curling across the trail, which blasted off the tree when the sap exploded. A strike from a previous year will have turned dark but will still be visible, as a long bare patch running up the tree with a furrow in the middle. If the tree lives long enough, new bark will grow across the scar.

Author crossing foot logs

BARBARA THWAITES

Avoid hiking during bear- and deer-hunting seasons, except on Sundays.

CLOTHING AND EQUIPMENT

The difference between a walker and a hiker is a day pack. A walker must obtain any required supplies along the way. If you are walking in town or at a shopping mall, this is actually possible, but when out in the country-side you had better take your supplies along with you. When you get thirsty, take out your canteen; when you get hungry, take out your lunch; when it starts to rain, take out your poncho; when the insects get annoying, take out your repellent; and when you get turned around, take out your map and compass. If it looks like you're going to spend an unexpected night in the woods (a late start is the easiest way to do this), take out two large plastic garbage bags. Make a hole in the bottom of one bag and put your head through it. Pull the other one up over your legs. You won't sleep much, but you'll be ready to go in the morning. Otherwise the bags will come in handy if you should find trash left by others.

There is a bewildering variety of day packs, but a good one should be made of nylon and have padded shoulder straps, some outside pockets, and a main compartment. Canvas or even leather would do, but these are heavier than nylon.

Today almost all canteens are plastic, which means that they can be placed in the freezer (allow room for ice to expand) to give you a supply of ice water in summer—although they can't be put on the stove to thaw out in winter. A lunch or snack should contain calories—lots of calories. On the trail, calories are food energy. Lightweight ponchos are made of plastic or coated nylon. A Gore-Tex parka can also provide warmth but will cost more. In winter a sitting pad of 6mm ensolite is worth its weight. A camera and binoculars are also useful, as is a book of animal tracks. The trouble is to keep the weight of your day pack down to only 4 or 5 kg.

All seasons are hiking seasons. In the warm months you will want to wear shorts and short-sleeved shirts, usually of cotton. The prime requirement is to be comfortable. In cooler weather, you will want to switch to long pants and long-sleeved shirts; in cold weather, wool or synthetic pile garments and even polypropylene underwear. If the ground is snow-covered, gaiters will close the gap between pants and boots, keeping snow out of your socks. In winter the soft beauty of summer is replaced by a harder aspect, but good country is beautiful year-round.

As Aldo Leopold wrote, "I am glad I shall never be young without wild country to be young in. Of what avail are forty freedoms without a blank spot on the map?"

HIKING BOOTS AND WALKING SHOES

Wet spots, sharp sticks, roots, and rocks grow wild along Pennsylvania's trails. (Hikers have too often been forced back onto those portions of the land that nobody else wants.) So proper footwear is required if you are to avoid unpleasant experiences or even injury. Hiking boots and walking shoes are the most specialized and expensive pieces of a hiker's equipment. Both must have good arch support at the very least.

Hiking boots come in a vast range of prices, and in general you get what you pay for. The cheapest are just glorified sneakers that provide little ankle support. Cheap hiking boots wear out a lot faster than higher-priced ones.

Medium-weight leather boots are all you are likely to need on Pennsylvania's trails. The fewer pieces of leather, the better: Most blisters seem to form at seams. Good boots will have lugged soles to give you better footing on the trail, and they will be moderately waterproof.

You may be able to get a lower price on boots by mail order, but good fit is critical. So go to an outdoor store. The clerks there will spoil you for shopping malls because they really know what they are selling. Fit your boots over the socks you will wear on the trail—frequently, a thin inner pair of polypropylene and a thick, mostly wool outer pair.

Walking shoes are low-cut with leather or fabric uppers and some sort of rubberlike sole. They do not provide ankle support and thus are suitable for day hiking on only the best of trails. It doesn't matter whether they are waterproof; since they are low-cut, rain and snow will have plenty of access.

BACKPACKING

Opportunities for backpacking in eastern Pennsylvania are limited to Delaware and Lackawanna State Forests, plus the heavily used Appalachian Trail. The Appalachian Trail is the longest trail in the state, but from PA 994 in the west to Totts Gap in the east it is almost entirely on state game lands. The Game Commission has a general ban on camping. Remember that hikers do not contribute to the Game Commission in any way unless they also hunt.

The Game Commission permits shelters along the AT as well as primitive camping. The rules for primitive camping are given here:

1. Camp within 60 meters of the AT.
2. Camp only 1 night at a given site.
3. Do *not* camp within 150 meters of a water source or road crossing.
4. *No* open fires during times of fire danger.

These rules seem quite generous—but the catch is that they apply only to through-hikers. You can hike from A to B, but not back to A. It's true that this rule is rarely enforced, but hikers get upset when it is. Be aware of this limitation if you choose to backpack the AT on game lands.

Trailside shelters concentrate the problems of heavy use. Except in winter, shelters should be avoided on Friday and Saturday nights. They are likely to be filled or they may attract local beer parties. You must either stop early or risk finding a shelter already filled beyond capacity.

That said, a good backpack on the Appalachian Trail is between Caledonia and Pine Grove Furnace State Parks. The distance is about 32 kilometers so it can be done as either a 2- or a 3-day trip. There are shelters at Quarry Gap, Birch Run, and Toms Run. See PATC Map 2-3. As yet no permits are required for backpacking the AT in Pennsylvania.

Backpack camping is permitted in Delaware State Forest along both Thunder Swamp and Blooming Grove Trails. Campsite locations are not designated but should be at least 15 meters from the trail and at least 100 meters from any road, building, water source, or wetland. A camping permit, still free, is required for all campers. Write to: Delaware State Forest, 474 Clearview Lane, Stroudsbug, PA 18360-3002 or call 717-424-3001. Permits may be faxed if time is short, but applications should ordinarily be made 10 days in advance. All three hikes on the Thunder Swamp

Trail plus the Blooming Grove hike could be converted to backpacks.

In Lackawanna State Forest, camping permits, still free, are required for all overnight stays along the Pinchot Trail. Write to Lackawanna State Forest, 401 Samters Building, 101 Penn Avenue, Scranton, PA 18503 or call 717-963-4561. Camping permits can also be obtained at Thornhurst Forest Foreman's Office just east of Thornhurst Picnic Area. Camp at least 15 meters from any trail and 100 meters from any drivable road. Both hikes on the Pinchot Trail could be converted to backpacks.

Be sure to practice minimum-impact camping. A considerable number of books have been written on the techniques of minimal- or zero-impact camping, but the best one is still Harvey Manning's *Backpacking One Step at a Time*. Manning is based in the Pacific Northwest, where the weather is even worse than Pennsylvania's.

ABOUT THIS BOOK

The description of each hike starts with a summary listing the location, the total distance hiked, the time required, the total amount of climbing, highlights along the way, and relevant maps. It should help you decide which hikes match your capabilities and the time available.

Hiking distance has been measured with a Rolatape Model 623m measuring wheel because trail distances are poorly known, except on the Appalachian Trail. Distances are given in kilometers because metrication has become a bottom-up procedure in this country. Metrication is too important to be left to leaders whose commitments are determined by the latest poll.

Hiking times are determined by SOAP (standard old-age pace). Young hikers will have no trouble shortening them, but bear in mind that hiking is not competitive: It is the quality of the experience that counts. These times do not include lengthy breaks.

Vertical rise is the total amount of climbing on the hike, which may exceed the difference between the highest and lowest points along the way. Vertical rise is determined from US Geological Survey (USGS) topographic maps. *Highlights* can be lakes, waterfalls, views, ghost towns, ruins, natural areas, or major trails. *Maps* lists the USGS topographic maps for the hike, plus other maps that may cover the area. Yes, there is a nice map of each hike provided in this book—but if you take a wrong turn, you may stray off the edge of it.

Directions to trailheads are given under "How to Get There," and are still given in miles. Some trailheads are on state routes ("SR," followed by four digits). These roads are paved but their quality is one level below that of regular state highways ("PA," followed by up to three digits). Inconspicuous signs bearing the state route number can be found at the ends of each road and at important junctions along the way. Beware: SR numbers change at county lines in an unpredictable fashion.

The hikes have been separated into five regions for convenience: South Mountain, bounded by the Mason-Dixon line, Cumberland Valley, and Susquehanna River; Saint Anthony's Wilderness; Philadelphia and vicinity, bounded by the Mason-Dixon line, Susquehanna and Delaware Rivers, and Blue Mountain; the Poconos, bounded by the Delaware and North Branch of the Susquehanna Rivers, Blue Mountain, and the New York boundary; and North Mountain, bounded by US 220, the New York line, and the North Branch of the Susquehanna River. (I have been generous to the Poconos and included parts of the Ridge and Valley Province with that region, but the Poconos are the best part of eastern Pennsylvania. Besides, the boundaries of the Ridge and Valley region are more complicated to describe.)

I've made every effort to devise circuit hikes, but this has not always been possible. In such cases the hike is described as an in-and-out hike or, if longer, as a car-shuttle hike. Car-shuttle hikes require two cars.

The trips here range from short walks, to half-day hikes (up to 8 km or 3 hours), to all-day hikes, to some real boot-busters (over 16 km). They cover virtually every type of terrain found in eastern Pennsylvania.

MAPS
State park maps: from individual park offices or
Bureau of State Parks
PO Box 8551
Harrisburg, PA 17105-8551
1-800-63-PARKS

State game lands (SGL) recreation maps:
Pennsylvania Game Commission
Dept. AR, 2001 Elmerton Avenue
Harrisburg, PA 17110 (50 cents per map)

Public-use maps for state forests: from individual state forest offices or
Bureau of Forestry
Department of Conservation and Natural Resources
PO Box 1467
Harrisburg, PA 17120

USGS maps:
Distribution Branch
US Geological Survey
Box 25286, Federal Center,
Building 41
Denver, CO 80225
303-202-4700 ($5 per map)

PATC maps:
Potomac Appalachian Trail Club
118 Park Street, S.E.
Vienna, VA 22180
Write or call 703-242-0315 for current prices.

TRAIL ORGANIZATIONS
Keystone Trails Association
PO Box 251
Cogan Station, PA 17728-0251
Membership is still only $9 a year. The four issues per year of the *KTA Newsletter* alone are worth several times the dues. Updates for hikes in this book will be given in the newsletter's "Hiker Alert" column. Visit the KTA Web site (http://www.reston.com/kta/kta.html).

Appalachian Trail Conference
PO Box 807
Harpers Ferry, WV 25425-0807

BOOKS
Pennsylvania Hiking Trails, 11th edition, 1993. Published by Keystone Trails Association, PO Box 251, Cogan Station, PA 17728, but available in all the better bookstores. Write for current price.

Roadside Geology of Pennsylvania, by Bradford B. Van Diver, 1990. Published by Mountain Press Publishing Company. This book will add greatly to your enjoyment of Pennsylvania's exciting geology. A lot happens when continents collide, and you can see much of it from Pennsylvania's trails.

Circuit Hikes in Virginia, West Virginia, Maryland, and Pennsylvania, 5th edition, 1994. Published by Potomac Appalachian Trail Club, 118 Park Street, S.E., Vienna, VA 22180.

Hiking Guide to Delaware Water Gap National Recreation Area, revised edition, by Nick Miskowski, 1994. Published by New York–New Jersey Trail Conference, GPO Box 2250, New York, NY 10116; 212-685-9699.

Gettysburg Heritage Trail Guide, 9th edition, by Costa Dillon and William Curtis, 1993. Published by Boy Scouts of America York-Adams Council.

KEY TO MAPS

——	main trail
• • •	side trail
Ⓟ	parking
⇈	view
⌂	shelter

SOUTH MOUNTAIN

1

Caledonia State Park

Location: 9 miles east of Chambersburg

Distance: 4.7 km (2.9 miles)

Time: 1¾ hours

Vertical rise: 175 meters (575 feet)

Highlights: relics of the charcoal iron era

Maps: USGS 7½' Caledonia Park; PATC map 2-3; park map

Caledonia Park was first opened as an amusement park by a trolley company, much as Pen Mar on the Maryland border was operated. Caledonia is named for a charcoal iron furnace operated by Thaddeus Stevens— abolitionist, statesman, and father of the public school system in Pennsylvania. The iron furnace operated from 1837 to a few days before the Battle of Gettysburg, in 1863, when it was destroyed by Confederate troops under Jubal Early.

In addition to the Appalachian Trail, there are 15 km of trails in the park. This circuit hike uses two trails in the eastern part of the park and adjacent lands of Michaux State Forest. These trails follow old charcoal roads and the millrace and, except for a short section between them, are relatively free of rocks, so walking shoes should be adequate.

How to Get There
Caledonia State Park is located at the junction of US 30 with PA 233 between Chambersburg and Gettysburg. This junction is 8.8 miles east of exit 6 off I-81, on US 30. You can park at the Iron Furnace Monument lot on PA 233 just north of US 30.

The Trail
Start your hike just to the left of the half-scale replica of the furnace stack on the Thaddeus Stevens Trail. Pass a junction with the Charcoal Hearth Trail, on which you will return, and cross a bridge over the millrace. The iron furnace was of the "cold blast" type, which required a waterwheel to operate the bellows. If the blast failed for any reason—which happened all too often—the furnace would cool off and its contents solidify. Then the entire stack would have to be rebuilt.

Cross the millrace, which still carries water, and continue along it. There are occasional yellow paint blazes.

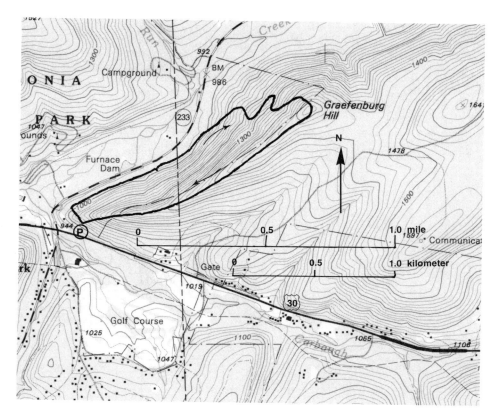

PA 233 is just to your left. Recross the millrace and continue on the Charcoal Hearth Trail, which is rough at first. Furnace Dam, which furnishes water to the millrace, is on the far side of PA 233. Next, pass the organized group camp and, at 1.4 km, bear right on a charcoal road that climbs Piney Mountain and draws away from PA 233.

A charcoal iron furnace required the charcoal from a hectare of forest every day it ran. Trees were cut, stripped of bark, and stacked on a flat piece of ground dug out of the mountainside. The pile was then covered over with leaves, earth, and sod to limit the air flow, and set on fire. Producing charcoal took anywhere from 1 to 4 weeks. The process required continuous attention, as the fire could either go out if it got too little air or turn the pile to worthless ash if it got too much. After cooling, the charcoal was transported by wagons along the charcoal roads, which were also built by hand.

First you will reach hearth 5, followed by number 4. Hearth 3 is on a side trail to your left. Then pass hearths 2 and 1. All are marked with signs. At 2.6 km you arrive at the 465-meter summit of Graefenburg Hill, marked by a post in the ground. Soon you encounter white blazes marking the boundary between Michaux State Forest and the park. This is a delightful ridgetop trail. Your path descends slowly and the noise from US 30 becomes louder. Turn left on the Thaddeus Stevens Trail at the bridge over the millrace and follow it

Millrace

back to your car.

Additional hiking at Caledonia can be found on the Ramble Trail, a short loop on both sides of Conococheague Creek in the western side of the park. Other loops are possible; see Hike 22 in *Circuit Hikes in Virginia, West Virginia, Maryland, and Pennsylvania.*

2

Pole Steeple

Location: 8 miles south of exit 11 off I-81

Distance: 8.7 km (5.4 miles)

Time: 3¼ hours

Vertical rise: 232 meters (760 feet)

Highlights: view, Appalachian Trail

Maps: USGS 7½' Dickinson; PATC map 2-3; park map

The famous Appalachian Trail (AT) passes through Pine Grove Furnace State Park on its way from Springer Mountain in Georgia to Mount Katahdin in Maine. The halfway point is just east of the park. In-season, look for through-hikers along this trail. They tend to be lean and have neat but worn-looking backpacks. If the temperature is much above freezing, they will be wearing shorts. Northbounders pass through Pine Grove Furnace in June, while southbounders don't get here until September.

This circuit hike uses the white-blazed Appalachian Trail, a blue-blazed side trail, and a dead-end but paved road. It visits a natural overlook above Laurel Lake called Pole Steeple. This quartzite cliff was named by Boy Scouts who planted a flagpole on top of it. The name persists, but the pole is long gone.

Pine Grove Furnace was a charcoal iron furnace that operated from 1837 to 1863. Operation of the ore pit that is now Fuller Lake continued until 1893, when the pit flooded. At most state park swimming areas the certain drowning depth is just above the knee, but at Fuller Lake the swimming area is 13 meters deep!

You will want your boots for this hike, as the AT footway is rocky and the descent through the cliffs at Pole Steeple is *very* rocky.

How to Get There
Pine Grove Furnace State Park is located on PA 233, 8.1 miles south of exit 11 off I-81 (between Carlisle and Shippensburg) and 13.5 miles northeast of US 30 at Caledonia. Proceed east on Hunters Run Road for 0.2 mile, then turn south into the Fuller Lake parking lot.

The Trail
Start your hike at the far corner of the parking lot. Immediately after passing the dressing stockade for the beach,

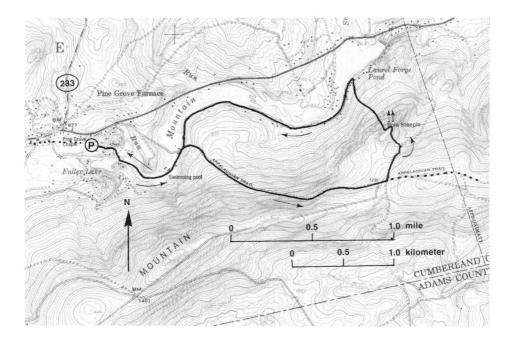

turn left on a gravel path. The white blazes proclaim that this is part of the Appalachian Trail. At the corner of a meadow is a confusing double blaze. Ignore it and continue on the gravel path past the food concession. Then cross bridges over Mountain Creek and the outlet from Fuller Lake.

Continue on a wide trail along Mountain Creek. This is the route of the South Mountain Railroad, which served the ironworks. This part of the AT is also open to bicycles.

At 0.8 km you pass the Swamp Trail, a loop trail to your right. Mountain Creek is on your left.

Turn right at 1.2 km and begin to climb Piney Mountain along the white blazes of the AT. Bicycles are not permitted beyond this point. Maine is ahead of you and Georgia behind. Soon you cross a meadow and reach the halfway point of the AT. Every time the AT is relocated, this point shifts north or south. Originally it was at Center Point Knob, a good day's hike north of here. About 80 percent of AT relocations are longer than the original trail.

Shortly after you reach the top of Piney Mountain, a couple of charcoal hearths are to your left. During the charcoal iron days, the entire South Mountain area was clear-cut repeatedly on a 20- to 25-year cycle to feed the iron furnaces. Next, pass an unblazed trail from your right.

Turn left on the blue-blazed Old Forge Road (not drivable) at 3.5 km. Continue past two unmarked trails to your left. Turn left on trail at 3.8 km and climb steeply to Pole Steeple, which turns out to be a quartzite cliff. Be careful, as there is quite an adequate drop to the rocks below. Before you is Laurel Lake, formed by a dam on Mountain Creek. Beyond is the main body of South Mountain.

If you're afraid of heights, the best course would be to retrace your steps

Cliffs at Pole Steeple

to the park. To continue the circuit, though, bear left to the spot where the blue blazes descend very steeply through a break in the cliffs. This break is actually a 300-million-year-old fault. The rocks moved along this zone as continents collided, and you can see the resulting polished surfaces called slickensides.

After entering the woods at the bottom of the cliffs, you pass several more charcoal hearths. Turn left on paved Railroad Road along the shore of Laurel Lake at 5.1 km. Mountain Creek is visible at several places. Along the way you pass the Ice House Trail, which crosses Mountain Creek, and at 7.5 km you close the loop. Continue ahead on the former railroad grade, now the Appalachian Trail, to return to your car.

Additional hiking opportunities at Pine Grove Furnace include Sunset Rocks (Hike 6).

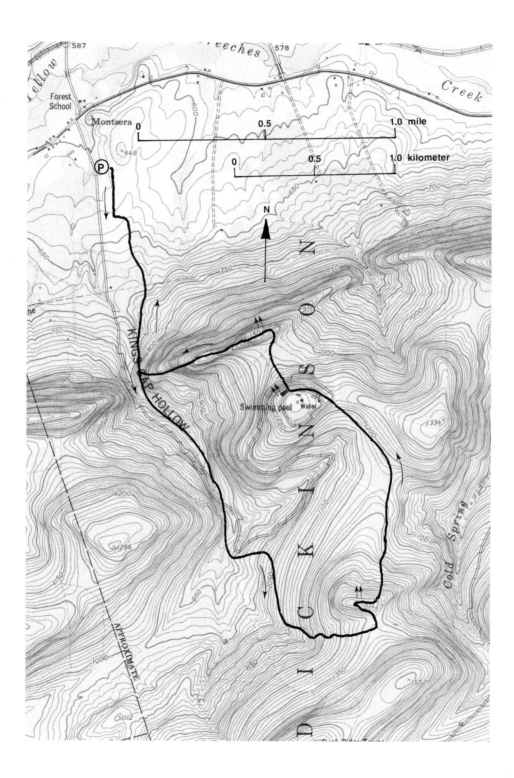

3

Kings Gap

Location: 5 miles southeast of exit 11 off I-81

Distance: 10.1 km (6.3 miles)

Time: 3¾ hours

Vertical rise: 340 meters (1115 feet)

Highlights: mountain stream, views

Maps: USGS 7½' Dickinson; park map

Kings Gap Environmental Education Center is located on the north edge of South Mountain in Cumberland County. Unlike a regular state park, this park's primary mission is education. Busloads of schoolchildren come to learn about the out-of-doors and Pennsylvania's natural heritage. I'm sure that any break from classroom routine seems like fun and the children are unaware of the painless education going on.

Starting in 1906, James Cameron, grandson of Simon Cameron—who served in the US Senate and as secretary of war to President Lincoln—began buying land here. The tract eventually reached 1100 hectares. He built the 32-room mansion at the top of the hill. Its architecture might be termed "bunker"—the house was furnished in haute hunting camp—but the view from its terrace across Cumberland Valley is unmatched. What a place to be lord of all you survey! James Cameron introduced conservation measures to restore the land, which had been abused by a century and a half of charcoal production for the local iron furnaces. Along this hike you can see how successful these efforts have been.

After Cameron's death in 1949, 580 hectares, including the 32-room "cottage," were purchased by Masland and Son Carpet Company of Carlisle, which used the mansion as a guest house. In 1973, with the aid of The Nature Conservancy, the Masland tract was acquired for the state.

You will want your boots for this hike due to the rocks and wet places along Kings Gap Hollow Run.

How to Get There

Kings Gap can be reached from exit 11 off I-81. Drive south on PA 233 for 2.5 miles, then east on SR 3006 for 2.3 miles. Turn south on Kings Gap Hollow Road. Kings Gap can also be reached from PA 34 just north of

Mount Holly Springs. Drive west on SR 3006 for 4.5 miles; then turn south.

On Kings Gap Hollow Road it is only 0.2 mile to the Pine Plantation Day-Use Area. Turn left to the parking lot. Thirty thousand pines were planted in this 17-hectare plot back in the 1950s. Pick up a copy of the trail map of Kings Gap, usually available at the display map.

The Trail
Make your way left behind the solar composting toilet, following the paved trail for handicapped access. Soon you come to a restored log cabin in a clearing. Leave the paved trail and pick up the red-blazed Rock Scree Trail, which follows a woods road straight through the plantation of Douglas fir, larch, and white pine—lots of white pine. The pine plantation is being thinned to permit continued growth.

Cross the Pine Plantation Trail; turn left between a vernal pond to your right and a stone wall to your left. Turn right and cross an unblazed trail. Climb past a charcoal hearth and, at 1.7 km, turn right on the blue-blazed Ridge Overlook Trail. Descend and turn left on the yellow-blazed Kings Gap Hollow Trail along the stream. Proceed upstream to a crossing of paved Kings Gap Hollow Road. Follow the Watershed Trail ahead, over a bridge and past a small pond. Continue through a stand of young white pines and bear left to a parking area. (The map said the Watershed Trail was blazed purple, but the blazes looked white to me.) Pass an open-air classroom and reach the parking lot at 3.3 km.

Cross the parking lot and pick up the orange-blazed Scenic Vista Trail. This trail was built and is maintained by the Susquehanna Appalachian Trail Club. The Scenic Vista Trail follows charcoal roads to 4.6 km, where you turn left on trail. After a climb you reach a view north over the Cumberland Valley. A stand of pitch pines frames the vista. Beyond, the trail descends through the woods, crossing an old swath and turning left to reach a power line. Turn left to a parking area on the paved road at 6.8 km.

The Scenic Vista Trail continues below the mansion (which is open to the public) to a junction with the Rock Scree Trail. To see the attractive view from the terrace, continue ahead on the Rock Scree Trail and then turn left up an unmarked path to the terrace. This view extends from Blue Mountain Tunnel in the west to Wagoners Gap in the east. Retrace your steps and continue down the Rock Scree Trail, crossing the paved road for the last time.

Next, cross the Forest Heritage Trail twice and continue on the Ridge Overlook Trail. The Rock Scree Trail diverges to your left; if the ridge is socked in with fog, you might want to stay on Rock Scree instead. At 7.8 km you reach a last view over the Cumberland Valley. Turn right on the Rock Scree Trail at 8.5 km and retrace your steps to your car.

This hike uses only 4 of the 12 trails at Kings Gap. Additional loops can be made on the Boundary and Watershed Trails, and on the Maple Hollow and Forest Heritage Trails—among others.

4

Gifford Pinchot State Park

Location: 10 miles south of Harrisburg

Distance: 11.1 km (6.9 miles)

Time: 3½ hours

Vertical rise: 80 meters (260 feet)

Highlights: Mason-Dixon Trail

Maps: USGS 7½' Wellsville, Dover; park map; Mason-Dixon Trail System map 2

Gifford Pinchot was a two-term governor of Pennsylvania. Appointed to be the first forester of the United States by President Theodore Roosevelt, he helped designate 200 million acres of public lands as national forest. He is regarded as one of the prime movers in the conservation movement. In Pennsylvania, Pinchot is regarded as a hero of conservation. There is even a chapter of the Sierra Club named after him. But in California Pinchot is remembered as a villain, because he permitted the damming of Hetch Hetchy, the second Yosemite Valley.

The fight to save Hetch Hetchy was led by John Muir himself, and the failure to protect this valley led directly to the formation of the Sierra Club, still one of the strongest conservation groups in the country.

As governor of Pennsylvania, Pinchot fostered a program to pave rural roads and "get the farmer out of the mud." "Pinchot Roads," as they were called, were hard surfaced and high crowned. The first such road is now PA 177, which now forms the northwest boundary of Gifford Pinchot State Park.

The Mason-Dixon Trail starts at the Brandywine Trail in Chadds Ford and heads south through Delaware and Maryland before heading north along the Susquehanna. It meets the Appalachian Trail at Whiskey Springs on South Mountain. There is little public land along it, and most of its route follows low-use public roads. One of the longest off-road sections is here in Gifford Pinchot State Park. It strings together several shorter trails, which you'll walk on this hike, as it passes through the park.

How to Get There
This is a car-shuttle hike. You can reach Gifford Pinchot Park from exit 15 off I-83; follow the signs for PA 177 south.

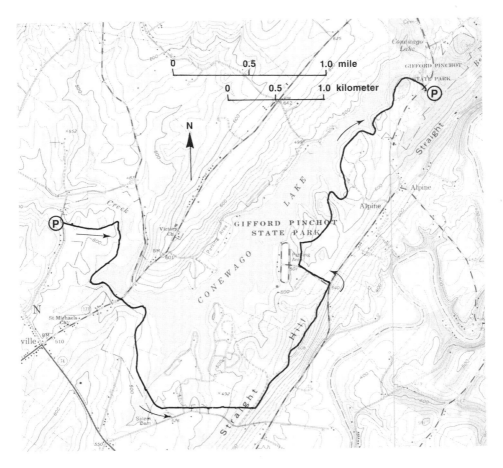

It is 5.9 miles to the park. Turn left on Alpine Road and proceed 0.5 mile to the dam. The Lake Side Trail emerges here. There is room for two or three cars to park here, but do not block the gate. If more space is needed, park at the overlook picnic area and add 200 meters on Alpine Road to your hike. Leave one car here.

Return to PA 177. Turn left and drive 3.5 miles to the traffic light in Rossville. Turn right onto PA 74. In just 0.3 mile, turn right onto Squire Gratz Road and go 0.6 mile to the Beaver Creek Trail and parking area.

You can also reach the park from York by heading northwest on PA 74;

and from Dillsburg (along US 15) by heading southeast on PA 74.

The Trail

Head into the woods on the Beaver Creek Trail, following the blue blazes. Turns are indicated by double blazes in which the upper blaze is displaced in the direction of the turn. The trail passes eastern red cedar, white oak, white pine, and shagbark hickory trees to reach the bank of Beaver Creek. At times you see old stone walls in the woods; these walls border fields that are now reverting to woods.

At 1.4 km you pass some ledges to your right and then more white pines.

Mason-Dixon Trail

These are followed by a short section of puncheon and a footbridge over an inlet. You reach boat-mooring area 1, with rest rooms, and cross PA 177 (use caution) at 2.5 km. Continue on the Mockingbird Trail, which leads to the shore of Pinchot Lake and then inland. There is plenty of poison ivy here.

Cross under a pole line at 3.3 km and continue along the park boundary. Traverse a stream as best you can at 4.0 km, and reach a paved road at 4.6 km. The contact station for the campground is visible to your left. Continue through the woods on a relocation that gets the trail off East Camp Area Road.

Turn left on the Ridge Trail at 5.6 km; continue past a junction with the Old Farm Trail to the left. Next you reach the Pinchot Trail. These junctions are marked with routed post signs.

At 7.1 km, turn left on paved road to the Conewago Day-Use Area. Pass a ball field to your right, then turn right past pavilion 1. Turn right on the Alpine Trail, and right again on an old woods road. Reach a junction with the Midland Trail at 8.1 km; continue ahead on Midland, crossing a footbridge, followed by the big climb of the day. Stay on the Midland Trail where the Fern Trail goes off to your right. Tulip trees grow along this section.

At 8.5 km turn right on Lake Side Trail North, and right again at the edge of the lake. Then pass a particularly well built old stone wall to reach another junction with the Fern Trail. Cross boat-mooring area 3 and jog right at a couple of picnic tables under a large spruce tree.

The trail continues along the lake; large boulders afford views across the water. At 11.8 km you reach the corner of the dam that forms Pinchot Lake. Proceed to Alpine Road and your car.

For additional hiking opportunities at Gifford Pinchot, you could explore a network of trails near the campground or a loop formed by the Quaker Race Trail and Lake Side Trail on the other side of the lake.

5

Gettysburg

Location: on US 15, about 5 miles
north of the Mason-Dixon Line

Distance: 13.0 km (8.1 miles)

Time: 5½ hours

Vertical rise: 140 meters (460 feet)

Highlights: Little Round Top,
Pickett's Charge

Maps: USGS 7½' Gettysburg,
Fairfield

*You've seen the TV series and the movie.
Enough of virtual reality. On this hike,
with just a tad of imagination you can
experience Gettysburg on your own as you
reenact Pickett's Charge or the defense of
Little Round Top.*

You might think there wouldn't be
an opportunity for hiking at a national
military park, but that's not the case.
Although in the 1860s soldiers were
sometimes carried on trains or boats
or rode horseback, they mostly moved
and fought on foot. You can get a
much better idea of what they faced if
you are on foot rather than in a car.

This hike is based on the Billy Yank
Trail in the *Gettysburg Heritage Trail*
Guide, published by the Boy Scouts
of America. The "Billy Yank" name is
not entirely accurate, as the route
takes you along both sides of the battle
line. The route visits Little Round
Top and the site of Pickett's Charge,
places where decisive actions took
place on the second and third days
of the Battle of Gettysburg. Despite
the monuments and markers that
pepper the landscape, it is still possible to feel something of what the
two armies experienced here for three
days in July 1863.

The battle resulted from Lee's invasion of the North in June following
his triumph at Chancellorsville. He
planned to threaten Harrisburg and
Philadelphia in order to draw the
Union Army into the field; he would
then destroy it in a defensive battle.
The threat to these cities was blunted
when the bridge over the Susquehanna
at Columbia was burned by the local
militia. While Lee's troops were for-
aging for supplies, they collided with
Union troops near the road hub
of Gettysburg. (With 10 or 11 roads,
Gettysburg was *the* road hub of southern Pennsylvania.) Along the way the
Confederates burned Thaddeus
Stevens's iron furnace at Caledonia
(see Hike 1).

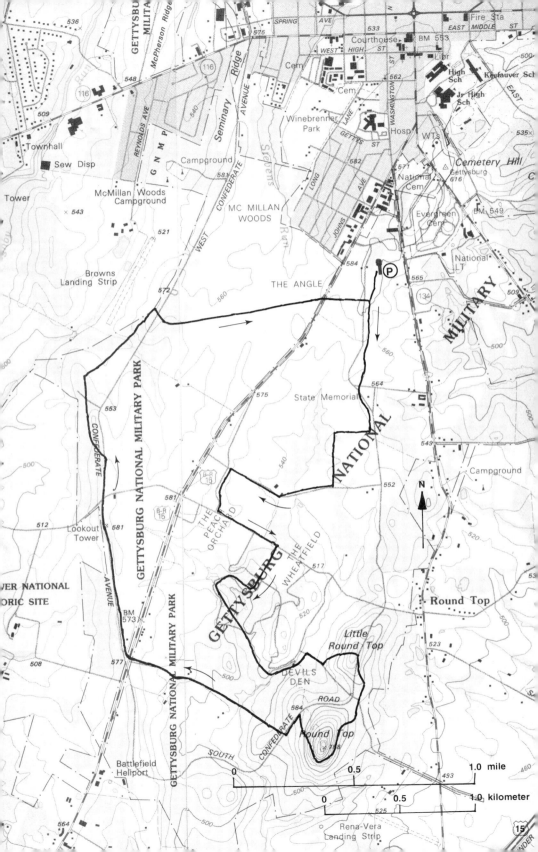

By July 2 the two armies were on parallel ridges south of Gettysburg. As you will see, these ridges are so low as to be barely discernible except at Big and Little Round Tops. (Lee's forces had carried the day on July 1, breaking the Union line north of town and driving the Federals back to the [...]. Along this [...] happened on

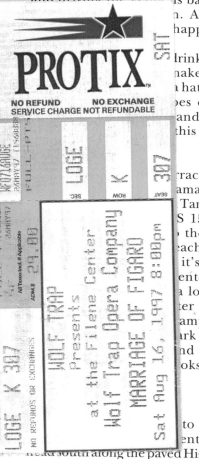

[...]rinking foun-[...]ake sure you [...] hat. You will [...]es or boots. [...] and a lot of [...] this hike.

[...]race on the [...]ama Center. [...] Tanneytown [...]S 15 for 2.9 [...] the visitors [...]ached from [...] it's about 1 [...] enter.

[...] lot, if pos-[...]er lot. Stop [...]amphlet for [...]rk map and [...]nd the *Heri-*[...]okstore ($1

[...] to the west [...] enter, then [...] south along the paved High Water Mark Trail. At 100 meters, bear right and continue south along Hancock Avenue. Look out for traffic. Note that the avenues were not here at the time of the battle; roads and pikes were here instead. The Angle—an offset in the stone wall—is to your right. You will return there late in the hike.

At 500 meters the paved High Wa-ter Mark Trail ends. Continue south toward the Pennsylvania monument. It is the largest one you will see. What would these monuments and memorials look like if Maya Lin had designed them?

Note the Tammany monument: It's the one with the tepee and a Native American wearing feathers. Some Native American units did fight for the Confederacy, west of the Mississippi. Pass the Pennsylvania monument and continue to the Minnesota monument: It's the one with a soldier running with a rifle. The 1st Minnesota suffered 65 percent casualties in the battle.

Turn right at the Minnesota monument and proceed across a field to a post-and-rail fence. Then turn left and follow the fence to United States Avenue. Turn right and pass General Sickles's headquarters. On July 2 Sickles advanced his Union corps beyond Cemetery Ridge, defying orders, inviting attack, and leaving Little Round Top undefended. The attack wasn't long in coming.

Now turn left on Sickles Avenue, and left again on Wheatfield Road. Continue on this road to a metal sign that says WHEATFIELD. Turn left across the Wheatfield. Two hours of fighting on July 2 left the field covered with bodies without giving either side an advantage.

When you hit a paved road (Sickles Avenue again), turn right and then left on De Trobriand Avenue. Follow De Trobriand past the monument for the 110th Pennsylvania to a metal sign that says DE TROBRIAND AVENUE. Turn left here and follow an old railroad grade. This was the bed of a trolley line built to bring an earlier generation of visitors to Devil's Den and Little Round Top. There are two footbridges along this section. Cross Brooke Avenue. The trolley grade comes to an end, but you continue across a footbridge over Plum (or Bloody) Run. At 5.2 km you reach a drinking fountain. Rest rooms are to your right and Devil's Den to your left.

Avoid a road to your right and continue straight ahead to Warren Avenue. Turn right and then pick a path up Little Round Top. From up here you get an idea of its strategic importance, which was realized late on July 2 by Brigadier General Warren (his statue overlooks Devil's Den). The Confederate attackers were beaten back, but just barely.

Beyond the top, make your way to the parking lot and turn right. After 150 meters, bear left on a paved path to the monument for the 20th Maine. Under the command of Joshua Lawrence Chamberlain, the 20th Maine repulsed a series of assaults that would have flanked Little Round Top. With ammunition exhausted, Chamberlain ordered a bayonet charge that routed the Rebel attackers. Lee had come within a whisker of winning the second day at Gettysburg.

To continue your hike, follow the path down to a small parking lot on Wright Avenue. Turn left on Wright and, after 40 meters, turn right on a horse trail. This leads up the slope of Big Round Top to a junction with the Loop Trail. Bear left on the Loop Trail, which is fitted with posts as a nature trail. (These posts can be interpreted with the sheet you picked up at the visitors center.) Big Round Top, although higher than Little Round Top, did not have the same strategic importance because it was wooded, then as now. Little Round Top had been cleared a few months before the battle.

Bear right on the Loop Trail at the next junction. At post 14 turn left, then left again on South Confederate Avenue. After 55 meters, turn right on a path next to a split-rail fence.

This takes you to Granite Farm and the end of a gravel road. Follow the gravel road to the junction of Confederate Avenue and Emmittsburg Road. Cross with care.

Turn right along West Confederate Avenue and follow it along the Confederate front line on Warfield Ridge, going by the Arkansas monument.

Pass the observation tower, then cross Millerstown Road. Continue north on West Confederate Avenue. After Pitzer Woods, turn left into the amphitheater parking lot. In-season there are drinking fountains here.

Keep left of the amphitheater and follow the horse trail through the woods. When the horse trail nears West Confederate Avenue again, look through the trees for the Virginia memorial topped with General Lee riding Traveler. Follow a path out to the avenue and pass by the memorial. This was the starting point of Pickett's Charge on July 3. It is 1.4 km to the Angle—and all in the open.

Fifteen thousand Confederates emerge from the trees and start across the fields. Their aiming point is that grove of trees you can see on Cemetery Ridge. They are faced by 9000 Federals.

Conventional military wisdom says the attacking force should have numbered at least 27,000. Why did Lee make such a mistake and depart from his game plan? As novelist and Civil War historian Shelby Foote has said, Lee's blood was up by this time. He had won the first day and had come so close on the second. His supplies were running low. One more attack could change the course of the war: Recognition of the Confederacy by England and France might follow.

Pickett's Charge was preceded by a 2-hour artillery duel. A German military observer called it a waste of powder. Follow the route of General Pickett's men toward the far rise. Imag-

General Robert E. Lee

ine that 9000 men are shooting at you.

At first the fire is cannons with explosive and solid shot. But as you approach, musket fire is added and the cannons switch to canister. Canister turns a cannon into a giant shotgun. With each shot, great gaps are torn in the advancing formation. A few men make it to the Federal line at the Angle. But there are not enough of them. They are killed or captured. The survivors stream back toward Seminary Ridge. Lee rides out to meet them. "My fault, my fault," he is saying.

General Meade's failure to counterattack or even pursue the Confederates led to the perception that Gettysburg ⟩

had been a Confederate victory. Vicksburg surrendered to Union forces on July 4, and it was thought that the South had broken even. Only later did it slowly become apparent that Gettysburg was not a victory for the South.

Nor was it a clear-cut victory for the North. The Confederate invasion had been turned back, but an opportunity to destroy Lee's army had been missed.

Continuing your hike, follow a paved pathway for the first 200 meters. From there you, unlike Pickett's men, must follow a path through the fields. Don't walk through any crops. (The fields were wheat in 1863; they are now milo, because wheat has proved irresistible to the overabundant deer herd in the park).

On the path, you will find a couple of missing rails in the fence next to Emmittsburg Road. Cross carefully. (Traffic was one hazard Pickett's men didn't have to face that day.) There is a gap in the fence on the other side. Follow the path to the Angle, cross the low stone wall, and continue across Hancock Avenue to the High Water Mark Trail. Bear left and make your way back to the Cyclorama Center.

After you've seen the museum, you can find additional hiking on the 5.6 km Johnny Reb Trail. See the *Gettysburg Heritage Trail Guide* for directions.

6

Sunset Rocks

Location: 8 miles south of exit 11 off I-81

Distance: 13.3 km (8.3 miles)

Time: 5 hours

Vertical rise: 323 meters (1060 feet)

Highlights: view

Maps: USGS 7½' Dickinson; PATC map 2-3

This hike on the famous Appalachian Trail (AT) and the Sunset Rocks side trail is based at Pine Grove Furnace State Park. The camp store at this park, which you will pass as you drive in, is the site of the half-gallon club. AT through-hikers are expected to buy, and consume on the spot, half a gallon of ice cream. Not to worry: Through-hikers expend 4000, 5000, or more calories per day and lose at least 10 kg along the way. Don't try this if you're not a through-hiker!

There are rocks, wet spots, stream crossings, and usually some mud along this hike, so you will want your hiking boots.

How to Get There

Pine Grove Furnace State Park is located on PA 233, 8.1 miles south of exit 11 off I-81 (found between Carlisle and Shippensburg). It is 13.5 miles northeast of US 30 at Caledonia State Park. From the north, turn right at the park office and then take the second left, passing the park store (formerly the stable of the old ironworks). Turn left twice again, passing the furnace stack and parking there. From the west, turn right on Bendersville Lane at the park boundary, passing the AYH hostel, formerly the ironmaster's mansion. Turn right and then left to reach the furnace stack. Avoid the area reserved for overnight hikers on the Appalachian Trail.

The Trail

From the furnace stack, follow the white blazes of the Appalachian Trail back across Bendersville Road and past the AYH hostel. Turn left on PA 233 for 175 meters (use caution) and then turn right on a gravel road. This is the AT, which climbs gently, passing several cabins and cottages. Continue climbing on a charcoal road. When the trail levels off, you pass several hearths where charcoal was made for the iron furnace back at Pine Grove. The trail becomes rockier, passing young white pines and then descending to an unsigned junction with the blue-blazed Sunset Rocks Trail at 2.7 km. You will return on this trail toward the end of this hike. For now, cross Toms Run on a footbridge and continue on Old Shippensburg Road. Farther along, this road is still passable to vehicles and is used to reach camps near the AT. At 3.1 km a side trail leads left to a spring.

There is a power line along this road. Where the power line turns right, so do you. Camp Michaux was once located to your left; in the 1930s, it was the first Civilian Conservation Corps camp in the state. During World War II it served as a prisoner-of-war camp; after the war it became a church camp. Many early meetings of the Keystone Trails Association were held here, before it was abandoned in 1972.

Now pass the stone ruins of a barn behind a fringe of spruce trees. This barn is said to have been built by Hessian prisoners during the Revolution.

Continue ahead on Old Shippensburg Road. At 4.3 km turn left on a gated old woods road. Red, white, and chestnut oaks grow along this section of the trail. In places there is an understory of white pines, which are not supposed to be shade tolerant.

Bear left and cross a stream as best you can. At 6.1 km you reach the Toms Run Shelters. Shelters are a tradition on the AT, dating back to the days of heavy canvas tents and frameless packs. Today there are over 200 such shelters along the trail. Building and maintaining them at remote sites such as this absorbs an enormous amount of volunteer effort: A new shelter may require 3000 volunteer days. It certainly is a great relief to reach a shelter after an all-day rain, but through-hikers must still carry a tent. The shelters are not evenly spaced along the AT, and there may be gaps of up to 50 km between them. When you do reach a shelter it may already be full, as they operate on a first-come, first-served basis. Further, the shelters have become magnets for trail problems. For instance, in theory occupancy is limited to a single night, but you may find a youth group that stays a fortnight. (It's a lot cheaper

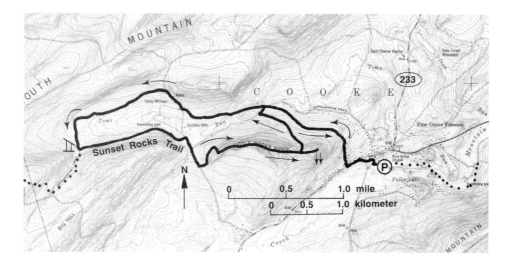

View from Sunset Rocks

for the group than going to a commercial summer camp.)

The Toms Run Shelters make a convenient place to stop for lunch. Then move on, crossing the outlet from a spring and then a bridge over Toms Run. Just beyond, turn left on the blue-blazed Sunset Rocks Trail. Again, there is no sign. (The AT is poorly signed—not because signs haven't been made and installed, but because they've been stolen or destroyed by vandals.)

Soon you cross a wet spot and then pass a clear-cut to your right that has grown into a thick stand of black birch. Beyond it is another cut to your left that has grown into red maple. Pass several charcoal flats, then continue on a logging road. At 7.3 km, bear right in a clearing. This junction is poorly blazed even when leaves are off the trees. Cross some wet areas and then turn right on paved Michaux Road.

After 300 meters, turn left on the *second* of two gravel roads. (The blazes are confusing at this point and seem to indicate a turn on the first side road.) Continue on the trail and circle a camp. The trail parallels the ridge before turning right and climbing to the crest of Little Rocky Ridge. As you proceed east, the path becomes a scramble over rock outcrops. Follow the blazes as best you can.

This ridge has a rugged beauty and is set about with white and pitch pines in addition to chestnut oaks. At 9.5 km you reach a trail junction in a sag. To reach the view, continue ahead to the east end of Little Rocky Ridge. You will be looking south and west.

Return to the sag and turn right (north) on the trail. Descend—steeply, at first—passing a stand of hemlocks to a junction with the AT at 10.5 km. Turn right on the AT and retrace your steps back to the park and your car.

Puncheon

7

Cumberland Valley

Location: between Carlisle and Mechanicsburg	
Distance: 16.5 km (10.3 miles)	
Time: 4¾ hours	
Vertical rise: 135 meters (450 feet)	
Highlights: rural Pennsylvania	
Maps: USGS 7½' Mechanicsburg, Carlisle, Wertzville; PATC map 1	

Cumberland Valley is the local name for the Great Valley of the Appalachians, running from Georgia to New York State. When the Appalachian Trail (AT) was first laid out back in the 1930s, the Cumberland Valley was completely rural. The AT was routed on unpaved roads across the valley, whose crossing is a matter of geographical necessity since South Mountain comes to an abrupt end just north of Dillsburg.

After World War II the valley began to change. Suburbs and industry spread out from Harrisburg and roads were paved. Much of the land remained rural but was hidden from the roads by a veneer of development. Traffic became fast and heavy. The AT experience was seriously eroded—despite people like the ice cream lady, who gave ice cream to passing hikers.

Volunteers enlisted the National Park Service as empowered under the National Scenic Trail Act to purchase a corridor of land to get the AT off the roads. Several alternative routes were investigated. The route finally selected follows Stony Ridge, which runs straight across the valley. One of the leaders of this effort was Craig Dunn of Camp Hill.

Stony Ridge results from a vertical layer of igneous rock (originally molten) called a *diabase dike*. This dike is also responsible for the "boiling springs" of Boiling Springs: The igneous rock is impervious to groundwater, forcing it to the surface.

Wear your boots for this hike as there are stones on Stony Ridge, and there may be a good deal of mud. Be sure to stick to the trail; the public-use corridor is only 30 meters wide in places. Don't expect the wilderness experience typical of the AT. This section has a charm all its own.

How to Get There
This is a car-shuttle hike, so you'll need two cars. Take exit 17 off I-81

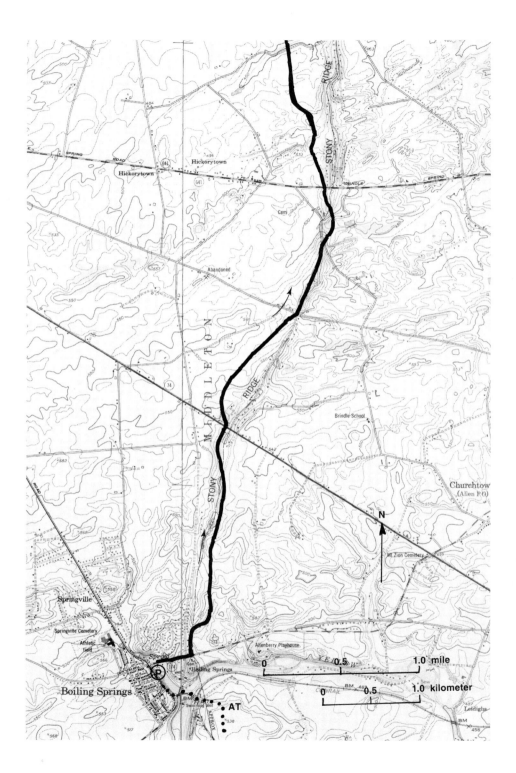

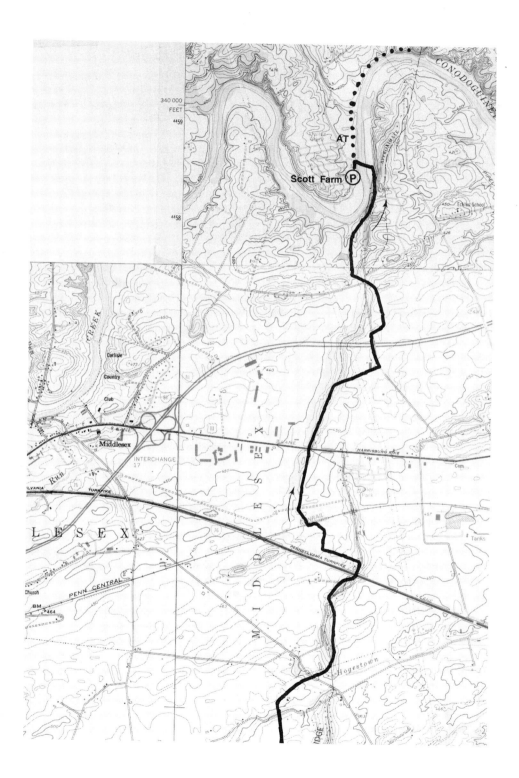

between Harrisburg and Carlisle. Head "south" on US 11. Immediately after the Budget Host Motel and across from Howard Johnson's, turn right onto Country Club Road. Drive east for 2.1 miles and turn left on Bernheisel Road at a T-junction. Drive north for 0.9 mile, crossing over Conodoguinet Creek. Then turn left into Scott Farm, the Mid-Atlantic Trail Crew headquarters. (Hiking is spoken here.)

Leave one car at Scott Farm and retrace your route to US 11. Turn right and get into the left lane as quickly as you can. After just 0.4 mile, turn left onto Middlesex Road at "Mature Fantasy." Drive south for 6.1 miles, crossing PA 641 at grade, zigzagging at Lisburn Road, and crossing PA 74 where the road name changes to South Ridge Road. At PA 174 turn right; 0.2 mile brings you to the Appalachian Trail Conference's Mid-Atlantic Regional Office across from Farmers Trust Bank. Turn left into the small parking lot. You may have to park elsewhere in Boiling Springs if this lot is full.

The Trail

From the ATC office, cross First Street (PA 174) and turn right. The 5 by 15 cm white blazes show that you are on the AT. Walk on the left, facing traffic, and climb the low hill, crossing South Ridge Road. After 400 meters turn left on a mowed path through a field of goldenrod. Some of these fields are returning to woods. Tens of thousands of pines and oaks have been planted by volunteers, to screen the AT from future development. The blazes are painted on wooden posts in the absence of both trees and large rocks.

At 1.1 km you enter a patch of woods, but soon you're back in the fields. Many of the fields on national park land are rented by farmers. Any appropriate, established use can be continued—growing corn or soybeans, or pasturing cows or horses. The intent is to preserve the agricultural character of the AT corridor.

The land is gently rolling and South Mountain, the southern edge of Cumberland Valley, can be seen behind you from the tops of rises. At several places farm roads cross the trail. It takes 7 or 8 days to mow the entire Cumberland Valley section of the AT. A lot more work is required to maintain a trail in the open than one in the woods. The trail must be mowed almost continuously during the growing season.

At 2.4 km you cross an old stone wall, and at 3.2 km you cross PA 74. Be careful. There is some parking on the far side. Then cross a stile over an electric fence and make your way across a horse pasture. Cross another stile at the far side of the pasture. (A stile is preferable to a gate in a fence, as it can't be left open.)

Trees along the trail are locust, walnut, both black cherry and chokecherry, mulberry, birch, and even a stray white pine.

Cross Lisburn Road at 4.8 km. Now turn right, enter woods, and turn left on an old paved road. At 5.8 km cross Boyer Road, which is also paved. Then cross a wet area and a bridge over a small stream. Cross PA 641 (Trindle Road) at 6.5 km. Again, be careful—lots of high-speed traffic. Cross Ridge Road, also paved, at 8.3 km, followed by a footbridge.

Next you pass a small pond, which may have wild ducks, and cross a footbridge over the outlet. Cross Old Stone House Road at 9.2 km and climb over a high stile. At the far edge of the field is a small cemetery—the Chambers (of Chambersburg) family cemetery.

Switchback up a rock slope at 10.0 km; cross another paved road; and cross an unpaved road. Then turn left on the next hard-surfaced road. Cross the Pennsylvania Turnpike on the road bridge at 10.7 km.

Turn left just beyond a house and follow the edge of a field to a crossing of the Conrail tracks. Do check for trains—although most of the heavy traffic is now on the roads. Continue through fields and woods, crossing US 11 on a footbridge at 12.6 km. (Before the AT relocation, hikers had to cross US 11 at grade.)

After more fields and woods, turn left on paved Bernheisel Road and cross I-81 on the road bridge at 14.1 km. Then bear right into a field. You come to the junction of Bernheisel and Country Club Roads at 14.8 km. Blue Mountain, the northern edge of Cumberland Valley, looms directly ahead.

Cross a stile into a cow pasture. Watch for blazes carefully here, as there are only a few of them. The blazed posts are circled by small fences to protect them from marauding cows.

After two more stiles turn right, cross a footbridge, and enter woods along Conodoguinet Creek. The AT is cut into the slope below Bernheisel Road. This is followed by a section of puncheon, which is occasionally rearranged or even swept away by floods.

At 16.3 km, turn left on Bernheisel Road and cross Conodoguinet Creek. Finally, turn left into Scott Farm, where you left one of your cars.

If development continues at its present rate, the AT corridor will soon be the only open green space left in the Cumberland Valley. If you would like to get involved in the efforts to maintain the AT experience, you can join the Cumberland Valley Appalachian Trail Management Association, PO Box 395, Boiling Springs, PA 17007.

Additional hiking opportunities can be found on the AT. To the north you can hike all the way to Mount Katahdin in Maine; to the south you can hike to Springer Mountain in Georgia.

SAINT
ANTHONY'S
WILDERNESS

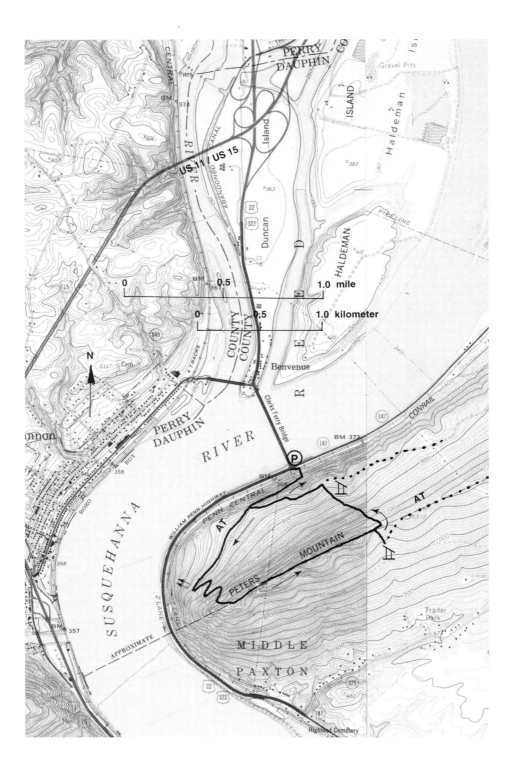

8

Peters Mountain

Location: north of Harrisburg, at the US 322 bridge over the Susquehanna

Distance: 7.6 km (4.7 miles)

Time: 4 hours

Vertical rise: 315 meters (1030 feet)

Highlights: views, AT shelters

Maps: USGS 7½' Halifax, Ducannon; KTA 7 & 8

Since the Appalachian Trail (AT) was completed in the mid-1930s, much of it has been relocated. Then there have been relocations of the relocations; in some places the trail has actually been relocated to its original route. On Peters Mountain you will see evidence of three different trail locations, each one better than the previous. The original location of the AT wasn't even on Peters Mountain, but on Blue Mountain just above Harrisburg. The Blue Mountain site required an extensive detour in order to cross the Susquehanna, so in 1955 the trail was relocated by Earl Shaffer, the first AT through-hiker, to cross on the Clarks Ferry Bridge.

There are only a few wet spots along this hike but there are rocks, lots of rocks, so wear your hiking boots.

How to Get There

The trailhead is at the south end of the Clarks Ferry Bridge (US 322) over the Susquehanna. From either direction, exit onto PA 147 and park off the pavement after you see the APPALACHIAN TRAIL sign. This point is 1.9 miles from the intersection of US 11/US 15 with US 322 on the far side of the river, at Amity Hall.

The Trail

Walk back to the APPALACHIAN TRAIL sign and follow the white blazes across the live railroad. Look for trains before you cross. Use the end of a stone wall as a stairway and continue through a couple of switchbacks, the first of which involves an old utility pole. When I saw this trail, its fine quality made me think it must have been built by the Mid-Atlantic Trail Crew—but it is the work of one man, Ron Gray, plus the occasional helpers he dragooned into service. Some rockwork farther on was done by the Mid-Atlantic Crew.

Note the poison ivy along the trail. Poison ivy is locally abundant on Peters Mountain. Locust, sassafras, maple, and red oak also grow here.

This section of the AT has already been reblazed in accordance with a new standard adopted by the Appalachian Trail Conference in July 1995 at its biennial meeting: Double blazes are used; at turns, the upper blaze is displaced in the direction that the trail takes.

Farther up, the AT follows the base of a ledge before finding a passage through it. There is an intersection on your left with the blue-blazed Susquehanna Trail, on which you will return. A few steps farther an unblazed trail leads right, to a previous location of the AT, which was too steep and started to erode. The signboards are still fixed to a tree on the old route.

Continue on the bench, passing a stone wall and, at 1.1 km, a stone foundation to the left of the trail. These are the remains of a farm here, on the bench halfway up Peters Mountain. Pass a spring and turn right on an old woods road.

At 1.6 km you reach a view over Duncannon, the Susquehanna, and Cove Mountain on the other side of this water gap. Now climb up the crest of the ridge on a series of switchbacks to some big rocks at 2.4 km. There is a view downstream from the top of the first big rock.

At the top of the ridge, continue on good footway to another view: At the point where the trail crosses to the other side of the ridge, you can see the Clarks Ferry Bridge. The rocks along the ridgetop are conglomerate, which looks like concrete because it is full of pebbles. Conglomerate is actually a very coarse sandstone. This is the Pocono sandstone of Mississippian age. Along with the Tuscarora and Pottsville sandstones, it is one of the chief ridge-formers in eastern Pennsylvania.

Ahead the ridge becomes a rockpile

and you must follow blazes carefully. This very rough section continues for 700 meters.

At 4.0 km you reach a junction with the blue-blazed Susquehanna Trail. Pass it by for now to visit the Clarks Ferry Shelter, built in 1987. The AT drops off the ridgetop. Turn right at a signed junction at 4.5 km and follow the obvious trail to the shelter.

This shelter is made of lumber and has a wooden floor, a shingle roof, bunks, a picnic table, and an outhouse, all set in a small clearing. This means you can dry your things—if the sun comes out. The Peters Mountain Shelter, built in 1994 on the other side of PA 225, makes this one look primitive. Peters Mountain is much larger, with a sleeping loft and a solar composting outhouse. Despite over 200 shelters along the AT, through-hikers must still carry tarps or tents. Sometimes shelters are filled beyond capacity, and there are gaps of up to 50 kilometers between them.

To continue your hike, walk back up to the AT and bear left. At the junction with the blue-blazed trail, turn sharply right along the ridgetop. At 5.2 km there is a very confusing intersection with an old route of the AT. A secret overseer has added incorrect blazes; they look newer than the correct ones. Turn sharply left at a stone cairn and start down the side of Peters Mountain. Although most side trails don't get the same level of care as the main AT, this one is fairly straight, which is helpful if you have to detour around blowdowns.

Reach the old Clarks Ferry Shelter at 5.7 km. It is built of locally grown logs with a dirt floor and a tin roof—albeit with a plastic skylight—and must have been built shortly after the 1955 relocation. The spring is off to the right.

Follow the blue blazes down to a

woods road and bear left on it. This woods road is also a former route of the AT. Cross the yellow-blazed national park boundary and continue on the sparsely blazed woods road to 6.3 km. (In many places the AT is now a long, skinny national park, maintained and managed by volunteers.)

Turn right on trail. Cross the swath of an old pole line, with another view of the Clarks Ferry Bridge. Continue along the top of a ledge to the break used by the AT. Here, turn sharply right and descend the impressive sidehill construction to PA 147 and your car.

For additional hiking on Peters Mountain, you could follow the AT farther "north" from the Clarks Ferry Shelter. The sidewalk on the Clarks Ferry Bridge is far safer than its predecessor, but I can't recommend it on aesthetic grounds: Monster trucks rumble right by your elbow.

Stone tower

9

Stone Tower Trail

Location: on PA 325 between
Dauphin and Tower City

Distance: 12.1 km (7.5 miles)

Time: 5½ hours

Vertical rise: 395 meters (1300 feet)

Highlights: large wild area

Maps: USGS 7½' Grantville, Lykens;
KTA 7 & 8

Just 20 kilometers north of the state capital is Saint Anthony's Wilderness, the second-largest roadless area in Pennsylvania. The origin and significance of the name are lost in time. It appears on maps from before the Revolution.

During the 19th century the area was a center of extractive industry. Coal mining, iron making, and logging left the ridges bare and the streams polluted with acid mine drainage. The area is haunted by ghost towns of that era (there are said to be over a thousand ghost towns in Pennsylvania), including Rattling Run, Yellow Springs, Gold Mine Gap Station, Cold Spring, and Rausch Gap. A standard-gauge railroad, the Schuylkill and Susquehanna (S&SRR), ran the length of Stony Valley between Second and Stony Mountains, linking these towns with the outside world.

As in much of Pennsylvania, this land was used and abused, but it has come back. The railroad is gone, forests again cover the ridges, and Stony Creek has been brought back to life by neutralizing the acid drainage with crushed limestone at Rausch Gap. Saint Anthony's Wilderness is now incorporated into State Game Lands 211; it stretches from near the Susquehanna east past Swatara Gap.

Sheer size makes Saint Anthony's Wilderness difficult to hike. Access from the south is restricted by private land and the Indiantown Gap Military Reservation, which uses the south side of Second Mountain as the impact area for artillery practice.

Access from PA 325 in Clarks Valley is limited by the De Hart Reservoir and Stony Mountain. The easiest access is from the ends of the S&SRR grade at Ellendale Forge and Gold Mine Road, or via the Appalachian Trail (AT) from Green Point on PA 443.

This is a short but rugged hike based on the PA 325 access. You will certainly want your hiking boots for the boulder slopes and a few wet spots. This should not be your first hike, as parts of it are rugged and there is a critical turn.

How to Get There
The trailhead is on PA 325, 5.0 miles east of the De Hart Dam. There is no trail sign, just a big red blaze on a tree facing west, but the trailhead is bracketed by small signs saying SR 325/370 on the west and SR 325/390 on the east. If you find a blue- or yellow-marked trailhead, you are too far east by 0.9 or 2.0 miles, respectively. There is parking space for only two cars at the trailhead, but there are more pulloffs in both directions along the highway.

The Trail
Head into the woods on the obvious footway, following neatly made red blazes. Turns use the offset double blaze adopted by the Appalachian Trail Conference in 1995; the upper blaze is displaced in the direction of the turn.

Cross Clark Creek, at 200 meters, on a log; there's a steel cable to hold on to. Boards have been nailed to the top of the log, improving the footing, but if you can't reach the cable you may have to ford the creek or get a companion to hold down the cable while you cross. Turn right on an old road at 700 meters. To the left this old road, on which you will return, is blazed pink.

At 1.1 km, turn left and climb on an old grade, passing the white-blazed boundary of Game Lands 211. Next, turn right on another old road that holds to the contour. Turn left on a log skid at 1.9 km for some serious climbing. The log skid evaporates after 100 meters and you bear right up a boulder scree, with occasional red blazes but no trace of footway. There

are only 110 meters of this scree slope before you reach the end of an old road, but there seem to be many more.

Turn right on the old road and continue to climb, passing a spring at 2.3 km. Note the dry stone walls on the side of this road; somebody put a lot of work into them but never finished— just another of the mysteries of Saint Anthony's Wilderness.

Swing left at the top of Stony Mountain to a junction with a blue-blazed trail at 3.3 km. Turn left. The red blazes continue to 3.5 km, where they turn right on a grassy bench among the workings of an old underground coal mine. The stone tower itself is partially hidden by trees. Beware: It looks as if it could collapse at any time. There is also an open vertical shaft. It is thought that the stone tower was used to create a draft, ventilating the mine shaft.

To continue your hike, follow the blue blazes down an old road to ruins of the ghost town of Yellow Springs. All that remain are piles of rock. Turn left on the white-blazed AT, passing more ruins, then a spring. At 7.3 km turn left on the blue-blazed Sand Spring Trail. There is a trail sign at this critical junction. Should you miss it, you may find an unmarked trail, right, to Cold Spring. Otherwise, you won't be sure something has gone wrong until the AT swings into Rausch Gap about 4 km from here.

Follow the Sand Spring Trail downhill and across the bright red waters of Rausch Creek. This is acid mine drainage, and it kills all life in the creek. At 7.8 km there is an unblazed side trail left, marked with a small wooden sign to THE GENERAL. The General (not included in this hike but only a 5-minute walk) turns out to be a rusting steam shovel used in coal

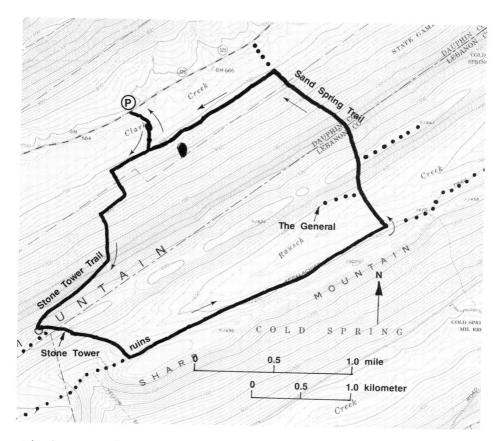

stripping operations.

Bear right on the blue blazes for some serious climbing over Pottsville sandstone boulders to the top of Stony Mountain, and a junction with a yellow-blazed trail to the right, at 8.2 km. A sign painted on a rock at this junction advertises SOUTH VIEW, a 10-minute walk down the ridge. On a clear day you can see all the way to Reading, but the Yellow Trail is a blazed bushwhack innocent of all traces of clearing. It is not included in this hike.

Instead, continue straight ahead, passing a large hemlock, and start down the boulder scree. At 8.4 km you reach the end of a log skid, and the going gets easier. Sometimes blowdowns or trees force the trail off the log skid into the rough, but for the most part the path sticks to the grade. Farther down, some of the blue blazes have faded to white; you don't reach the game lands boundary, though, until 9.4 km.

Turn left on the pink-blazed old road at 9.9 km. Sand Spring, a box spring set in moss-covered rocks, is within 20 meters of this junction. (You could reach PA 325 from here by staying with the blue blazes and rock-hopping across Clark Creek, but this would lead you to 1.4 km of tedious walking along the paved highway.)

Along the pink trail, pass a small boulder scree. You will reach the junction with the Stone Tower Trail at 11.4 km. Turn right at the red blazes and follow them back across Clark Creek to PA 325, your starting point.

You can find additional hiking in Saint Anthony's Wilderness on the yellow-blazed trail you crossed or on a loop west of the De Hart Dam. Follow the AT up Stony Mountain to a junction with the Horse Shoe Trail; follow the Horse Shoe west to the Water Tank Trail. Turn right and follow either of two versions of the Water Tank Trail down Third Mountain. Then turn right again on a blue-blazed trail that leads you back to the AT. See the KTA map, sections 7 and 8.

10

Rausch Gap

Location: on Gold Mine Road between PA 443 and PA 325

Distance: 15.8 km (9.8 miles)

Time: 5 hours

Vertical rise: 215 meters (710 feet)

Highlights: large wild area

Maps: USGS 7½' Tower City, Indiantown Gap; KTA 7 & 8

Saint Anthony's Wilderness, just 20 km north of Harrisburg, is the second-largest roadless area in the state. Today it is protected within the 17,000 hectares of State Game Lands 211. Here the Appalachian Trail (AT) has its longest section in Pennsylvania without crossing a road. Saint Anthony's Wilderness is laced with old trails and roads, most of them unmarked, unmaintained, and unmapped.

In the 19th century, Stony Creek Valley and Third Mountain were busy with industrial activity. Iron was smelted, coal was mined, and trees were logged. The area was dotted with towns—only ghosts remain today— many of which were connected to the outside world by the Schuylkill and

Susquehanna Railroad (S&SRR). This railroad grade is now used by the Pennsylvania Game Commission as a management road across Game Lands 211. The S&SRR grade is closed to auto traffic but open to bicycles.

There are rocks and wet spots on this hike, of course, so wear your boots.

How to Get There

The trailhead for this circuit hike is on Gold Mine Road toward the eastern end of Game Lands 211. From the south take PA 443 to Gold Mine Road, near Murray; follow Gold Mine Road over Second Mountain for 2.9 miles. From its junction with PA 325—about 1 mile west of Tower City—follow Gold Mine Road over Stony and Sharp Mountains for 4.3 miles. In either case, turn west on the old S&SRR grade at a GAME LANDS sign; park between the sign and the gate.

The Trail

Head back out to Gold Mine Road and turn left. Cross Evening Branch and bear left on a gated road. This old road climbs up Gold Mine Gap in Sharp Mountain. It seems unlikely that anyone ever mined honest gold here. They did mine anthracite coal; one story is that this was called "black gold."

At 1.4 km, avoid a railroad grade to

the left. Continue ahead, then bear left and cross Gold Mine Run. Don't try to negotiate the remaining timbers of the bridge; instead, descend the bank and scramble up the far side. The trail now traverses a stand of hemlock. The climbing eases off when you reach a plantation of red pine, spruce, and white pine on a bony pile. "Bony" consists of the worthless but highly acidic layers next to the coal, which were removed during mining operations.

At 2.6 km, an old road comes in from the right. You bear left, climbing again and passing some old mine works. Then pass a meadow to the left. You are now following a stagecoach road that once ran among the communities in this high valley between Sharp and Stony Mountains.

Pass a spring at 5.1 km and soon cross a stream. There is evidence that the trail is used by horses, but most use appears to come from mountain bikers. The bicyclists pile logs on each side of blowdowns so that they can ride right over them. The old stagecoach trail is easy to follow except at a couple of spots where piles of blowdowns have been detoured around.

At 6.1 km, jog left on the Penn Fuel Gas pipeline. In 30 meters the trail returns to the stage road, avoiding another pile of blowdowns. At 7.3 km you reach some old earthworks that were part of a coal mine. Bear right, off the grade, and follow red, yellow, and orange spray-paint blazes and orange flagging. Follow blazes carefully, as they twist and turn. (If you continued ahead on the old grade, you would see some of the worst acid mine drainage you are ever likely to encounter. Presumably it comes from an old underground mine.)

Cross the east branch and then the

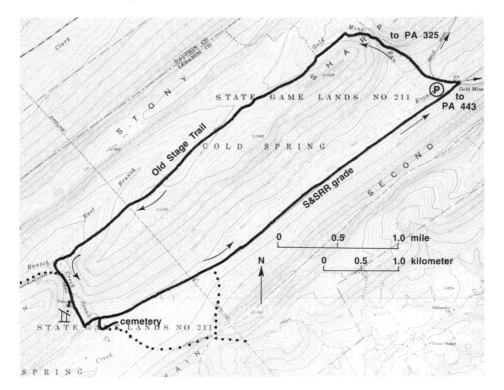

Through-hikers on the AT

main branch of Rausch Creek. Head downstream, crossing more acid mine drainage, and then bear left on the white-blazed Appalachian Trail. Bear right on a blue-blazed side trail at 7.7 km if you want to see the Rausch Gap Shelter (included in this hike). At one time Rausch Gap was the Hilton of the AT, but it has had its 15 minutes of fame. Other shelters are newer and more elaborate. Return along the same trail and turn right on the AT.

Turn left on the S&SRR grade at 8.4 km and cross the old railroad bridge over Rausch Creek. Note the water-treatment facility, which controls the acid mine drainage and permits fish to live in Stony Creek. Here Rausch Creek is passed through a bed of crushed limestone. You'll see a pile of fresh limestone—consumed in the process—behind a tree.

Immediately beyond the bridge, turn right on the AT to visit the old Rausch Gap cemetery (also in this hike). Note the old stone walls along the trail, ruins of the village of Rausch Gap.

Continue straight ahead where the AT bears right, and reach the cemetery at 9.8 km. Note that the graves are still tended. Small American and British flags are placed on them. The men who died in 1854 came from England; the child may have been born in Rausch Gap. Cemeteries and trash heaps are sometimes the most durable remains of ghost towns.

Return to the S&SRR grade and turn right. Cross the Penn Fuel Gas pipeline at 11.7 km, and pass a junction with Middle Patch Pass a little farther along. The S&SRR grade is a green tunnel through hemlock, white pine, and black birch. You will pass other trails, roads, and ponds before reaching the gate and parking lot.

Lengthy hikes are required to explore the vastness of Saint Anthony's Wilderness. A hike to Stone Tower on Stony Mountain is described in Hike 9 of this book. The AT runs for 23.5 km across SGL 211, although you can hike it in a day by using a car shuttle from PA 325 to PA 443 at Green Point.

PHILADELPHIA
AND VICINITY

BARBARA THWAITES

Henry's Woods Trail

11

Jacobsburg

Location: 10 miles north of Easton

Distance: 4.0 km (2.5 miles)

Time: 1¾ hours

Vertical rise: 65 meters (215 feet)

Highlights: hemlock glen, views

Maps: USGS 7½' Wind Gap; park map

Jacobsburg Environmental Education Center is on PA 33 between Wind Gap and Easton but close to Allentown and Bethlehem. It has 20 km of trails, about half of which are equestrian. Jacobsburg was named after a colonial village. Since its opening in 1985, it has provided a basic education in conservation principles for students within a radius of 40 kilometers.

The footway on this short hike is excellent, so walking shoes are fine.

How to Get There
Take the Belfast exit off PA 33. Follow signs to the junction of Henry and Belfast Roads, about 0.2 mile. Turn left on Belfast Road at the stop sign and follow it for 0.8 mile to a parking lot on the left, just beyond Bushkill Creek. There is a map board at the kiosk and trail maps of the center as well.

The Trail
Find the unsigned Homestead Trail at the right-hand corner of the parking lot near Belfast Road and start your hike there. Pass some walnut trees and continue on a mowed path through a meadow. Raspberries grow along the path, but poison ivy also thrives. There are bluebird houses in the meadow. (Watch for bluebirds flying around.) Ignore a trail from the left and continue into woods. Next, bear right at a set of posts blocking vehicular access. Look for deer in the fields along the Homestead Trail.

Continue under some power lines, and turn left next to paved Jacobsburg Road. Ignore a path to the right in the next meadow, and pass some sassafras trees. The meadows at Jacobsburg are old fields in various stages of reverting to woods. Larger trees grow along the old fencerows. Note the old apple trees along the trail.

After you pass some old field junipers, turn right and continue along the edge of a meadow. Walk by some more wooden posts and turn right along the edge of another meadow at the

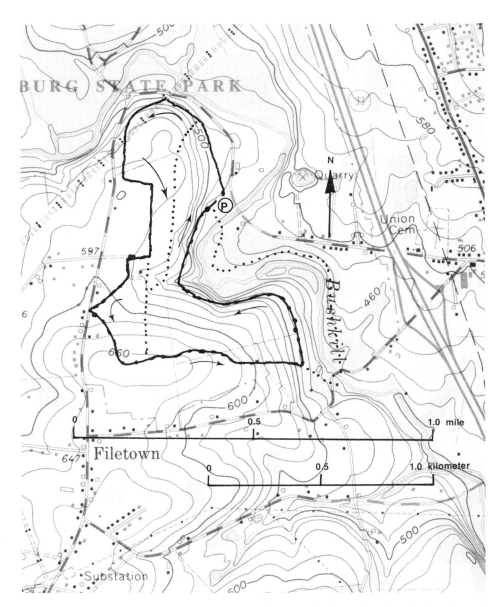

top of the hill. There are views across Bushkill Valley; on a clear day you should be able to see Blue Mountain.

Reenter the woods and reach a trail junction at 2.0 km. Bear right and then turn left, avoiding a trail ahead to Jacobsburg Road. Next, turn left at the edge of power lines. Trees along the wooded sections include ash and hickory. You can hear many birdcalls—the Homestead Trail is reputed to be the best for bird-watching at Jacobsburg Center, where 103 species have been reported. Turn left at the next two trail junctions, reaching the Henry's Woods Trail at 3.1 km.

If you wish to see the Henry homestead for which the trail is named (not included in this hike), bear right and follow the Henry's Woods Trail out to Henry Road.

This hike turns left, though, on the Henry's Woods Trail (which the park map calls the Toth Ridge Trail). Disregard the mysterious warning about the alleged hazards of this trail; the luxuriant poison ivy edging on parts of the Homestead Trail is more hazardous to most hikers than an occasional root in this path. The sidehill construction here is of high quality. Okay, there are a couple of roots. Note the honeysuckle growing along the trail.

Descend into a hemlock grove above Bushkill Creek. This is the most beautiful trail at the center. Cross a bridge over a dry run and then descend a flight of wooden steps. You will reach the amphitheater; the parking lot is just beyond.

You can extend this hike by crossing the bridge over Bushkill Creek, next to the parking lot, and following Henry's Run Trail downstream. Then recross the creek and follow the Homestead Trail. There are many options along the Homestead Trail, so you could avoid rehiking most of the trail you just completed. Avoid the Jacobsburg Trail, however, because of noise pollution from PA 33.

12

High Rocks

Location: near the Delaware River, between Washington Crossing and Easton

Distance: 4.3 km (2.7 miles)

Time: 1½ hours

Vertical rise: 60 meters (200 feet)

Highlights: views

Maps: USGS 7½' Lumberville; map board at Ralph Stover State Park

This short hike links Tohickon Valley County Park with Ralph Stover State Park. Ralph Stover himself operated a waterpowered grain mill here back in the 18th century. His heirs gave the park to the state in 1931. The High Rocks area was donated by James Michener, the famous author. Facilities at Stover Park were built by the federal Works Progress Administration during the Great Depression.

This hike is so short that it could be done as an in-and-out hike rather than a car-shuttle hike. The distance would increase to 8.6 km (5.4 miles).

How to Get There
Ralph Stover Park is located 2.2 miles from Point Pleasant (which is on PA 32) via Tohickon Hill and State Park Roads. You can also reach it from PA 413 south of Pipersville by following Stump Road (there is a sign) for 2.5 miles. Leave one car in the lot beyond the park office. The map board on the side of this building is not entirely accurate: At Tohickon Valley County Park, the trail actually leaves from the Deer Wood Campground, not the swimming pool area.

In your other car, head back down State Park and Tohickon Hill Roads to PA 32 in Point Pleasant. Turn left, cross Tohickon Creek, and turn left again on Cafferty Road just before the church. It is 1.3 miles to the Deer Wood Campground. If the group camps are not in use, park along the campground road. If they are in use, leave your car back at Tohickon Park itself and walk on Cafferty to the Deer Wood group camps. Add 400 meters to the hike's total distance.

The Trail
The trail enters the woods at the far corner of the field. It is spray-paint-blazed with red squares inside a white border. It starts out as just a beaten path but soon picks up an old road grade. At 530 meters, bear right and cross a couple of intermittent streams.

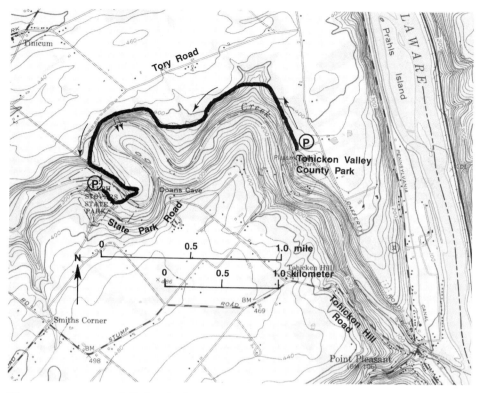

Then cross a waterfall that is dry most of the time. There is a fair amount of up and down on this trail.

Pass a stone wall to your right at 1.9 km; then bear left where an unmarked trail comes in from your right. Cross another intermittent stream to reach Dan's Overlook at 2.6 km. Dan's Overlook has a steel railing. There are truly formidable cliffs, some 70 meters high, below this and the other overlooks. Rock climbers use these cliffs; beware—there may be climbers below you. Next is Cedar Overlook, which also has a steel railing. Then come Balcony and, finally, Arquillite Overlooks. From these rocks you can see both up and down Tohickon Creek Valley.

The high cliffs were formed by Tohickon Creek eroding the rocks on the outside of a bend. Beyond the last overlook, cross a small bridge and turn left on trail. From here on the trail is marked with white blazes.

Cross a couple of intermittent streams. Turn left on Stover Park Road at 3.2 km and descend. The trail shown on the Stover Park map board as ahead of you no longer exists, due to lack of maintenance. The road soon enters private land, but it is closed to through traffic.

At 3.9 km you cross the bridge over Tohickon Creek (also closed to auto traffic). Then turn right and cross a bridge over the millrace. Stover's Mill was located here; the millrace brought water from the dam to power the mill. Continue upstream between the mill-race and Tohickon Creek to the dam. Then cross a bridge over the millrace and make your way to the parking lot and your car.

Additional hiking opportunities can be found nearby on the Delaware Canal towpath; see Hike 25.

13

Middle Creek

Location: 15 miles north of Lancaster

Distance: 5.3 km (3.3 miles)

Time: 2 hours

Vertical rise: 130 meters (490 feet)

Highlights: view, stream

Maps: USGS 7½' Womelsdorf, Richland; SGL 46 map 2

Middle Creek Wildlife Area was created primarily for one species—Canada geese. Over 250 other species of birds have been identified at Middle Creek as well, though. It is a birder's paradise. Middle Creek was dammed at a gap through the Furnace Hills, creating habitat for waterfowl. The balance of State Game Lands 46 is located on the Furnace Hills. Habitat doesn't have big brown eyes, but it's what really counts for wildlife.

The Horse Shoe Trail follows these hills across Middle Creek, and together with an old road and an abandoned trolley line it makes a small circuit hike on the east end of Black Oak Ridge.

A number of picnic areas are also provided on the 2532 hectares of

Middle Creek Wildlife Area, as well as a national-park-quality visitors center along the main road. Both Project 70 and Project 500 funds were used in the development of this area.

There are plenty of rocks and wet places, so wear your boots. There is also a lot of poison ivy along this hike.

How to Get There
The trailhead is on Hopeland Road (SR 2013), 3.1 miles south of the Hopeland/PA 897 intersection in Kleinfeltersville. You can also reach Middle Creek from US 322 at the village of Clay. Park along the road just north of the bridge over Middle Creek.

The Trail
Begin by heading up the yellow-blazed Horse Shoe Trail on the west side of the road. Soon you pass through a timber stand improvement cut. The haul roads have been seeded. At 700 meters you reach a junction with the Valley View Trail, which leads over the ridge and down to the Green Briar Picnic Area in about 1 km. The view over the wetlands is about 300 meters from this junction (not included in this hike). The Valley View Trail is marked with yellow metal triangles with one corner painted black; it is

for foot travel only.

Continue up the Horse Shoe to a steel-pylon power line at 0.9 km. There is a view left across Middle Creek Gap. Beyond the power line, turn right on an eroded old road that soon becomes a jeep road. Note that horses are permitted on this trail—but they would have to be very surefooted to negotiate the trail from the road to this point. This is the top of the hill. Next, you will see a food plot for game through the trees to your left; ordinarily, there isn't much for wildlife to eat in a mature forest.

At 1.5 km there is a view to the north across the power-line clearing. Turn left on the Elders Run Trail at the bottom of the saddle, 1.9 km from the road. Note the spruce trees growing here.

Elders Run Trail is an old road gated to motor vehicles but open to horses. At 2.2 km there is an old stone springhouse to the right of the trail. Years ago, one of the shelters along the Horse Shoe Trail was located near this point. Shelters hold a magnetic attraction for vandals, but the Elders Run Shelter seems to have survived until as recently as 1987.

Farther along, you pass a cleared area that was probably a log landing. Then keep right on the main road to 3.3 km, where you cross a bridge over Elders Run. At 3.5 km turn sharply left on the Middle Creek Trail, which appears to be an old railroad grade. Actually, it is an old trolley line that ran from Lancaster to Myerstown. This is now a foot-travel-only trail.

After repeated views of rapids in Middle Creek, cross a footbridge over Elders Run. A house on private land is visible on the far side of Middle Creek. Traverse a section of corduroy and pass a piped spring to the left of the trail at 4.4 km. Then pass under the power line and cross a couple of bridges, followed by a well-worn run-

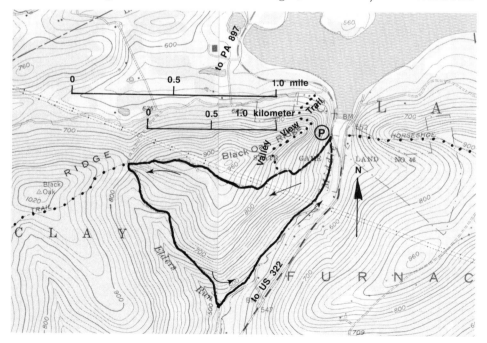

around (due to uncleared blowdowns on the old trolley grade). One more bridge and you are back at your car.

You can find additional hiking opportunities at Middle Creek on the Conservation and Willow Point Trails, both of which are quite short. Avoid the Deer Path Trail between the Red Rock and White Oak Picnic Areas unless it has been reopened.

There is also a short circuit hike east of Middle Creek. Climb the Millstone Trail from the White Oak Picnic Area, walking past the millstone to the vista over the lake. Head away from the vista and turn left on an unmarked trail that leads to the Horse Shoe Trail. Turn right on the Horse Shoe and follow it downhill to Middle Creek Gap. Turn right again on Millstone Road and follow it back to the White Oak Picnic Area.

Finally, you could follow the Horse Shoe Trail to the west, to either Segloch Road or Fox Road; both options require a car shuttle.

14

Susquehannock State Park

Location: 20 miles south of Lancaster	
Distance: 5.6 km (3.5 miles)	
Time: 2¼ hours	
Vertical rise: 220 meters (720 feet)	
Highlights: views, rhododendron	
Maps: USGS 7½' Holtwood; map in park map	

Susquehannock State Park, overlooking the lower Susquehanna River, is well developed for hiking, with 8 km of trails on only 91 hectares. This little-known park was listed by the Bureau of Parks as one of the 30 best-kept secrets of Pennsylvania's state parks. These parks are the least visited in the state. I find many of my favorites on this list.

You will find a map board of the park's trail system at one corner of the parking lot. The trails are coded with a rainbow of colors including yellow, red, green, pink, beige, and magenta. On my first visit it appeared to me that the chromatically challenged were in for a tough time. Not to worry: There are no blazes of any color on the trails, so you are no worse off than anybody else in following them!

A problem with unmarked trails is that different people have different ideas of where the trail ought to go. If enough people are of the same mind, then a switchback may be cut off or a dead-end trail produced if people go straight where they should have turned. If you find yourself on a dead-end trail, turn back and try again.

Some of the trails above Wissler Run are steep, rocky, and slippery, so you will want your boots for this short hike.

How to Get There

Susquehannock Park can be reached by driving south 4.1 miles from PA 372 on Susquehannock Drive. Then turn right at a sign for the park and go 0.8 mile to a parking lot just beyond the Landis House.

The Trail

Walk between the old Landis House and the park office. Pick up the Rhododendron Trail near some rest rooms. Trail junctions are usually marked with post signs. At a junction, turn right on the Five Points Trail and follow it over a footbridge. Then bear left uphill.

Wissler Run

Along the trail you pass tulip, black gum, beech, black birch, chestnut oak, and wild holly. A small tree with big leaves growing luxuriantly along the trail is the pawpaw, which appears to be extending its range north from the Mason-Dixon line.

Next, turn left near the Five Points corner, where five different properties come together, and pass through dense stands of rhododendron. Some of the shrubs appear to have died in the drought of 1995.

At 1.4 km, turn left along Wissler Run and immediately cross a side stream. Then turn right on the Rhododendron Trail and climb steeply. At 2.0 km, turn left and continue climbing past tall banks of rhododendron (in bloom around the last week of June and the first week of July). Ignore a trail that goes ahead, as it doesn't go very far. At 2.4 km, ignore another trail to your right. The Rhododendron Trail climbs and descends frequently. Along this section note several stands of dead hemlocks that have been cut down. Presumably they were killed by the woolly adelgid.

Then, at 2.5 km, switchback to your left on an old grade and climb again, ignoring yet another trail to your right. At 2.7 km turn right on the Fire Trail and follow it to an overlook above Wissler Run. This view is north to the Norman Wood Bridge, Lock 12 historic area, and the Muddy Run pump storage plant.

Now turn back and climb on an old road to a picnic area with rest rooms. Keep right to another overlook at Hawk Point. The cliffs below you are over 100 meters high. From here you can see some of the islands in the reservoir formed by the Conowingo Dam downstream in Maryland, as well as the Peach Bottom nuclear power station on the west side of the river. Mount

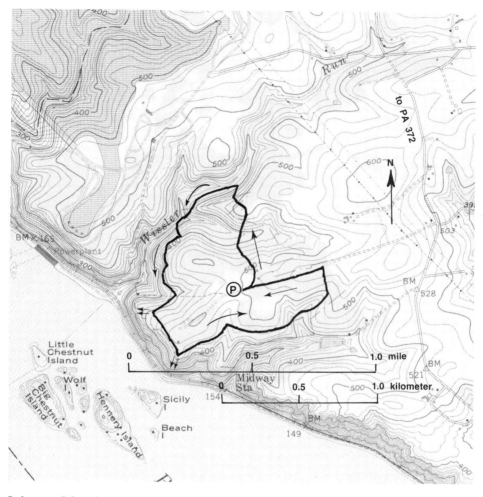

Johnson Island was the first bald eagle sanctuary in the world.

From Hawk Point, proceed to a small parking lot, then continue on the Overlook Trail. At 3.8 km, turn right on the Landis Trail; shortly after, ignore a trail to your right. Next, turn right on the Chimney Trail. At 4.6 km continue ahead on the Chimney Trail. The post sign is set wrong (or has been turned), and the trail that it indicates actually leads downhill to the park boundary.

Reach the end of the Pipe Line Trail and continue ahead on the Chimney Trail to the park road at 5.1 km. Turn left, and it is a short walk back to the parking lot and your car.

This hike has used 5.6 of the 8 kilometers of trail at Susquehannock State Park, so your best bet for additional hiking would be at the Holtwood Recreation Area, to the north of PA 372 (see Hike 20).

15

Nolde Forest

Location: 2 miles south of Reading	
Distance: 5.8 km (3.6 miles)	
Time: 2½ hours	
Vertical rise: 146 meters (480 feet)	
Highlights: evergreen plantations, stream	
Maps: USGS 7½' Reading; park map	

Jacob Nolde made his money in hosiery and, in the early 20th century, purchased 270 hectares of land on the hills south of Reading. At that time unproductive farmland covered the hills. Inspired by a single "pasture pine," Nolde hired an Austrian forester, William Kohout, and set about creating his own Black Forest with evergreen plantations of Douglas fir, Norway spruce, and Japanese larch, along with white, red, ponderosa, and Scotch pines. About 100,000 seedlings were planted per year for some 15 years. Mixed hardwoods—beech, oaks, tulip, and red maple—also grow here now.

Nolde Forest was purchased by the state in the late 1960s, using Project 70 money; it was closed to hunting and turned into an environmental education center. On a given day, several school classes will be participating in environmental studies. Any break from the usual classroom routine must afford a painless path to learning. And the students think it's just a great field trip.

The trails along this hike are mostly old fire roads with an excellent footway, so walking shoes are fine for this hike. In fact, you could probably push a stroller on many of these trails. The hike is arranged as a figure 8; you could shorten it by walking only one of the loops.

How to Get There
Nolde Forest is located on PA 625, just 2.0 miles south of the junction with PA 724. Turn at the main entrance road and drive 0.5 mile to a parking lot near the mansion.

The Trail
Turn back down the entrance road and bear left on another road closed to traffic. This road descends into the valley of Punches Run. Turn left at a teaching station and bear left on the Watershed Trail. Look out for poison ivy. The trails at Nolde are not blazed, but there are signposts at many inter-

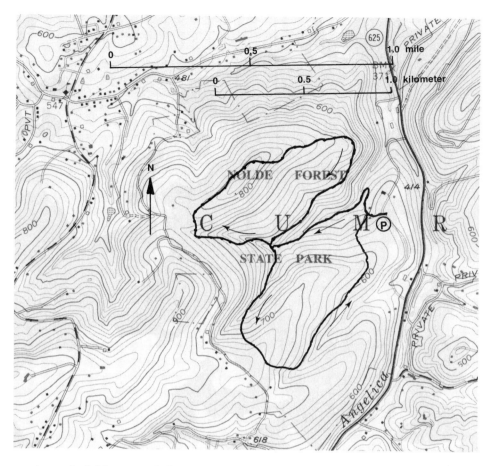

sections. At 0.8 km turn left on a road; bear right at the next junction. Jog left over a bridge at 1.1 km and continue up the Watershed Trail.

At 1.4 km, the trail has relocated itself to get around a pile of blowdowns that have not been removed. Rejoin the old trail next to a springhouse. Pass among several smaller springhouses and turn right on the Apple Tree Trail. (The park map is slightly in error at this point.) Then turn right on the Spruce Trail, and left on the Boulevard. Continue climbing gently to the top of the ridge.

In addition to the evergreen plantations, maple, oak, and tulip trees grow along your route. At 2.9 km there is a side trail to a rock outcrop; this hike swings right and continues on the Boulevard, which descends gently. At 3.6 km you reach a picnic area with rest rooms. The well here is no longer operational, but this is a good place for a lunch stop.

If you wish to truncate your hike, you can do so just beyond by turning left on the Boulevard or the Watershed Trail and retracing your steps to your car. To continue this hike, though, turn right up the Cabin Hollow Trail. The trail climbs gently through a stand of hemlocks that appear to be dying from the woolly adelgid.

At the top of the hill, cross Laurel Path and continue on the Owl Trail through a stand of white pines. Along this section you may hear a flock of crows making a great fuss. They are probably "mobbing" an owl because they know what owls do to crows at night.

Cross Middle Road and, at 4.8 km, turn left on Kissinger Road. At 5.5 km, just before Middle Road, turn right and continue downhill to the parking lot.

There are 10 kilometers of trails at Nolde Forest not used by this hike. Additional hiking opportunities in the Reading area can also be found at Blue Marsh Lake, north of town (Hike 27), and French Creek State Park, to the east (Hikes 22 and 26).

16

Ridley Creek

Location: 6 miles northwest of Media	
Distance: 6.9 km (4.3 miles)	
Time: 2½ hours	
Vertical rise: 150 meters (490 feet)	
Highlights: a pleasant walk in the woods	
Maps: USGS 7½' Media; park map	

Only 26 km from the center of Philadelphia is an oasis of peace and quiet. Except for an occasional jet or helicopter, the roar of traffic is absent and the silence is broken only by birdcalls. Ridley Creek is one of our newer state parks, purchased in the 1960s with Project 70 funds. Its 1000 hectares contain over 950 picnic tables; it sometimes gets really busy on a summer weekend. The park is gently rolling and occupies both banks of Ridley Creek. Some parts consist of fields reverting to woods, and others are mature timber.

Ridley Creek Park is closed to small-game hunting but it does have a con-trolled deer hunt in-season. (Large areas of many Pennsylvania state parks are open to hunting.) The principal trail is a paved multiuse trail forming an 8 km loop, which is used by walkers, joggers, and bicyclists. Horses are permitted in the northwest portion of the park. In addition, there are four conventional hiking trails—blazed white, yellow, blue, and red—on which bicycles are prohibited.

This hike is a circuit on the white trail. Walking shoes are adequate, except at the wettest times of the year.

How to Get There
The park can be reached from Gradyville Road; it is about 2.5 miles west of Newton Square. Or you can take PA 3 to either PA 352 or PA 252. Both these roads intersect Gradyville Road; from PA 352 you will drive east on Gradyville to reach the park, and from PA 252 you will drive west. The park can also be reached directly from PA 3 west of Newton Square via Sandy Flash Drive North.

To reach the trailhead for this hike, turn from Gradyville onto Sandy Flash Drive South and go 1.8 miles south. Pass the park office and follow signs to trailhead parking area 17.

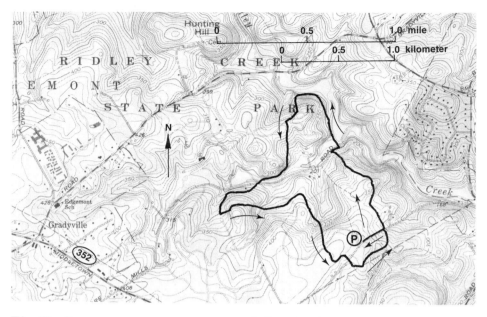

The Trail

From parking area 17, make your way to the fitness court, then to the multi-use trail beyond. Turn left and walk 300 meters, then turn left again onto the white-blazed trail. There are no trail signs here, but many junctions are marked by posts banded with the appropriate color. Where two trails use the same path, both color blazes are used. Within a few steps the yellow-blazed trail turns left to area 17; you could use it to avoid the multiuse trail, if you prefer.

At 500 meters, the red-blazed trail joins from your left before turning off on its own. Next, you cross the yellow-marked trail and pass some large rocks. Just before you reach the multiuse trail, the blue-blazed trail comes in from your left. Turn right on the multiuse trail for a short bit, then left on the white-marked trail along Ridley Creek itself. Cross a side stream on a bridge and continue up Ridley Creek. The trails all appear to be well maintained and are wide and easy to follow. In the mature forests you pass tulip, beech, ironwood, black gum, maple, and oak trees.

The trail then swings away from the creek and climbs to Picnic Area 9 at 2.6 km, which has rest rooms, picnic tables, and a parking lot. Walk out the access road. There are some white blazes on the pavement to direct you. Then turn left through a field that is revegetating with locust, crabapples, and multiflora roses.

Cross the yellow-blazed trail at the top of a ridge and descend, crossing a pipeline. Turn right on the multiuse trail and pass through a culvert under Sandy Flash Drive. Immediately beyond, turn left. Ahead is a confusing section where two white-blazed trails turn right. Keep left at both junctions. Continue past large tulip trees. On a bright day in the fall, with the footway covered with colored leaves, this is an especially delightful trail.

At 4.2 km cross a stream and a road. Then climb over a hill and cross Sandy Flash Drive at Picnic Area 16, with the usual facilities but only a couple of picnic tables. Beyond, the blue-blazed trail joins from your left; you cross the red-marked trail before the blue turns off to your right.

At 5.5 km, cross the road for the last time and continue through the woods on a sunken road. This is a particularly attractive section. Turn left up some steps and pass through a culvert under the multiuse trail. Turn left where the yellow-marked trail goes right (to the Tyler Arboretum). Next, you reach the multiuse trail. Turn left and return to parking area 17.

There are additional hiking opportunities at Ridley Creek on the multiuse, yellow, blue, and red trails, as well as at the adjacent Tyler Arboretum (see Hike 24).

17

Skippack Creek Trail

Location: 6 miles north of Norristown

Distance: 7.5 km (4.7 miles)

Time: 2¾ hours

Vertical rise: 100 meters (320 feet)

Highlights: creek

Maps: USGS 7½' Collegeville; park map

Evansburg State Park, in Montgomery County, the site of this hike, ought to be one of the Thirty Best-Kept Secrets of Pennsylvania's State Parks. It is all but impossible to find, even with the park map in hand. I did not find any signs until we were *in* the park, and these said only STATE PARK—NO ROADSIDE PARKING. This is the most low-profile state park I've ever visited.

But Evansburg is worth the effort to find. It has Skippack Creek, a free-flowing stream; a loop trail; a youth hostel; over 50 pre-Revolutionary structures; and the usual picnic area and equestrian trail. (Bicycles are prohibited on all hiking and equestrian trails.) Evansburg is an island of quiet on the fringes of Philadelphia.

The park was purchased as open space with Project 70 funds. The loop hiking trail was built by volunteers from a local chapter of the Appalachian Mountain Club. Many parks would be bereft of hiking trails were it not for volunteers.

How to Get There

Evansburg State Park can be reached from exit 31 off the Pennsylvania Turnpike. Turn east on PA 63. Where PA 63 turns left, continue straight ahead to a junction with PA 363. Turn right and drive 8.7 miles; then turn right on Germantown Pike at a traffic light. After 2.7 more miles, and immediately beyond the Eight Arch Bridge over Skippack Creek, turn right. This is Skippack Creek Road. Follow it to Mill Road and continue into the park on May Hall Road. Park near the picnic pavilion.

You can also reach the park from PA 113 south of Skippack Village by driving east on Mill Road; and you can reach it from US 422 via PA 29 and Germantown Pike. There are also parking areas on Anders Road and Water Street that you could use as starting points.

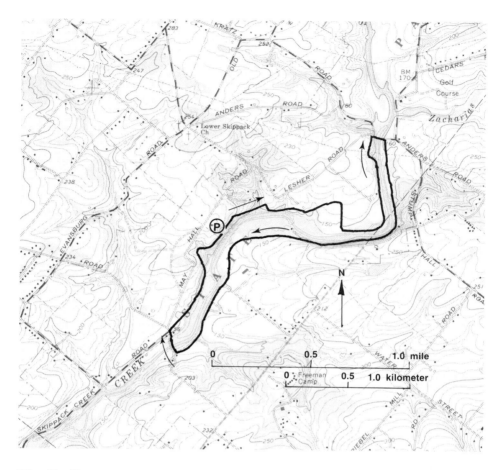

The Trail

From the rest rooms at the picnic area, head toward the creek and turn left along the edge of the bank. Skippack Creek is at the bottom of the slope. The trail is marked with diamond-shaped dirty white blazes. At 300 meters, bear right downhill. The trail ahead goes to the Nature Center. Exhibits along the way show that you are on part of the Nature Trail. One tells you about poison ivy, which is abundant in the park.

Cross the first of many footbridges. At 600 meters pass a junction with the Old Farmstead Trail. Cross another footbridge. The Horse Trail comes in from your left and the two trails continue together for 100 meters until the footpath bears left. Then pass the Diehl House, vintage 1855, on your left.

The trail emerges briefly at the edge of a field but reenters the woods in 10 meters along the edge of Skippack Creek. Listen for the rattle of the king-fisher along the creek. As you cross a high-water cutoff of the creek, note the low cliffs on the far side at the foot of Hemlock Slope.

At 2.1 km pass the Isaac Cassel House, dating from 1771. Then climb the bank and bear right on an old road. Next, pass under a power line where the Horse Trail diverges to your left. Turn right on Anders Road and cross Skippack Creek on the stone bridge. The bridge is closed to traffic, as parts of the upstream side are missing.

Now turn right on trail and pass under the power line again. Sycamore and beech trees grow along here. At 3.5 km, turn left and climb Hemlock Slope, passing a new house to your left. Be careful on Hemlock Slope: You saw the cliffs from the other side of the creek. Then cross over the highest footbridge yet. Next, you come to a series of quarries that make the going a bit tougher. Note the poison ivy growing here.

Beyond Hemlock Slope you cross the Horse Trail twice, and then a couple of footbridges. At 5.5 km, continue ahead on paved Water Street Road. The trail bears right along the creek bank but has to return to the road to cross a bridge over a side stream.

Turn right and cross the Iron Bridge at 6.3 km. This bridge is also closed to traffic. Turn right on the far side and pass a house dating from 1753. Cross the millrace from Markley Hill, built in the 1750s, and continue above it.

Pass a large spruce and evergreen plantation to your left. After crossing a stream and another footbridge, you are back in the picnic area. Turn left to the parking lot.

18

Wissahickon Gorge

Location: north-central Philadelphia

Distance: 7.6 km (4.7 miles)

Time: 3 hours

Vertical rise: 140 meters (460 feet)

Highlights: covered bridge

Maps: USGS 7½' Germantown; Wissahickon Valley Map

Fairmount Park in Philadelphia, the site for this hike, is the largest municipal park of any city in the world. The southernmost portion contains the Philadelphia Museum of Art, with the famous *Rocky* steps. For hikers, the best part is Wissahickon Gorge, in the northernmost part of the park. The gorge is about 10 km long and steep sided, though of modest depth. In addition to the main gorge, there are side valleys that penetrate far into the surrounding city.

At one time the gorge was a center of industrial activity, due to the presence of waterpower. Many dams were built to power grist-, saw-, paper-, and textile mills. When the steam engine replaced waterpower in the middle of

the 19th century, the city acquired the land.

There are a great many trails in Fairmount Park, most of them on old roads and grades. The mill owners lived on top of the gorge, and many of the roads were built for them to commute to work. Some of these trails are blazed but others are not. Forbidden Drive (forbidden only to motor vehicles), mostly on the west side of the Wissahickon, is an old carriage road along the creek itself. It is heavily used by joggers, dog walkers, bicyclists, horseback riders, and anglers. The eastern side of the gorge has more rugged trails on its steep slopes.

You will see on this hike that water is the enemy of trails. Some have been eroded to bedrock. The solution is to get water off the trails, and many water bars have been built of wood and stone by volunteers for this purpose. The volunteers wage a constant struggle to keep these water bars cleared and in good repair. If even a single rock is removed from a water bar, its usefulness is destroyed, because the water can then continue down the trail rather than being shunted off to the side. Perhaps some of these trails should be paved, and others closed.

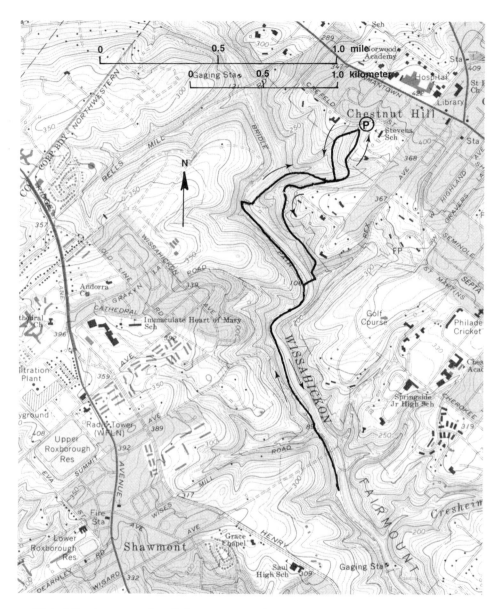

This hike is a sample of the attractions of the Wissahickon Gorge, but do not hike alone. Take a friend or a dog. The Wissahickon has its share of urban problems.

How to Get There

Despite its size, the Wissahickon Gorge is difficult to reach. There are only three parking lots—one at the Valley Green Inn, another at Kitchen's Lane, and one on Bell's Mill Road—and they may be filled, even in midweek. This hike uses a different access point.

From exit 25 off the Pennsylvania Turnpike, follow Germantown Pike east. Keep right immediately after the tollbooths. Drive south into Philadel-

Valley Green Inn

phia, about 4 miles. At the city limits, the pike becomes an avenue. One block after Bell's Mill Road, turn right onto Hampton Road, then left onto Crefeld Street. Crefeld swings left opposite house number 8917. The iron fence on your right looks like it belongs to a private estate but is actually the boundary of Fairmount Park. Park along the street.

Reaching this trailhead from elsewhere in the city may be more complicated. See any map of Philadelphia; there's one on the back of the official Pennsylvania road map.

The Trail

Near the far end of the iron fence there is a gate between two stone pillars. This is your entrance to the park. Please leave the gate closed. Bear right on a lavender-blazed trail that descends along an intermittent stream. After 300 meters, turn left on an unblazed trail and cross a bridge over Crefeld Creek. Bear left, uphill, briefly on the lavender-marked trail, then turn

sharply right on an unblazed trail.

Next, turn right on a white-blazed trail that comes in from Towanda Avenue. There is a stone wall opposite, along the edge of private land. After passing a bench, bear left downhill and turn left up some steps. At 1.6 km cross a bridge; beyond, there is a statue of a Native American crouching on a rock. The statue is said to represent Tedyuscung, a Lenni-Lenape chief (1720–63), but apparently the sculptor intended it to show a generic Native American.

Switchback downhill, then turn right on an unblazed old road that leads to the Rex Avenue Bridge over the Wissahickon River. This stone bridge was built by the Works Progress Administration during the Great Depression. On the far side turn left onto Forbidden Drive and proceed downstream, passing a derelict storm shelter, then a dam. Bear left on a road open to automobiles. Pass a parking lot and reach the Valley Green Inn, the only surviving inn along the

Wissahickon, at 3.9 km. Meals, maps, and rest rooms are available here. On raw days there may be a roaring fire inside to warm up by.

Then turn back upstream, passing the Rex Avenue Bridge to a covered bridge at 6.2 km. Cross it, and turn left on an orange-blazed trail. Climb over rough trail, ignoring a steep trail that comes down from your right. Next, bear right onto an unblazed trail where the orange-blazed goes left to Bell's Mill Road. The unmarked trail swings right to Crefeld Creek, passing cascades and then joining the lavender-blazed trail. Continue climbing, briefly retracing your earlier route, but this time sticking with the lavender-marked trail. Cross a stone bridge. A chain-link fence to your right marks the boundary of private land. Soon you are back at the gate to Crefeld Street.

There are plenty of additional hiking opportunities in Wissahickon Gorge. You may wish to become one of the volunteers who maintain these trails by joining Friends of the Wissahickon, Box 4068, Philadelphia, PA 19118. A map, "Roads, Paths, and Places of Interest in the Wissahickon Valley," is published by Friends of the Wissahickon; it can be obtained from them or from Way-to Go (215-483-7387), 4363 Main Street, Philadelphia, PA 19127.

19

Valley Forge

Location: near the junction of I-76 and US 422 north of Philadelphia

Distance: 7.8 km (4.9 miles)

Time: 3 hours

Vertical rise: 85 meters (280 feet)

Highlights: historical site

Maps: USGS 7½' Valley Forge; park map

Valley Forge is a shrine to our nationhood. It was here, in the winter of 1777–78, that the Revolution hit bottom for colonial forces. After a repulse at Germantown, the Continental army went into winter camp at Valley Forge. The site was both defensible and close enough to Philadelphia to keep an eye on the British there. Over the winter the force of 12,000 dwindled to 6000 through death, desertion, and expired enlistments. (Of the 2000 deaths, only one grave has been identified.) Rations and munitions were scarce to nonexistent. It looked like the end of the Revolution was near.

No battles were fought at Valley Forge. The British, snug in Philadel-phia for the winter, never attacked. They didn't have to. His Majesty's troops dined well on food bought with British gold. Colonial soldiers could pay only in paper money "not worth a Continental." The colonial troops, weakened by near starvation (one soldier wrote that on some days his ration was 1 gill of rice, some days 2 ounces of meat, other days nothing) and the cold (many soldiers endured the winter with disintegrating clothes and no shoes or socks at all), fell prey to typhoid, typhus, dysentery, and smallpox.

And yet it was here, at Valley Forge, that the war turned around. The army that marched out in June 1778 had reached 20,000 and was better trained and equipped. Five more years of war lay ahead, but conditions were never again as bad as they were here.

The emphasis in this park is on historical interpretation, not hiking, but there are still some opportunities for those who would rather see the park on foot than through a car window. It might seem that the ideal time for this hike would be April, when the redbud and dogwood are in bloom, but to really get a taste of the place you should come (without breakfast) on a bleak day in February.

Hut at Valley Forge

How to Get There

Valley Forge can be reached from exit 24 off the Pennsylvania Turnpike. Follow signs 1.6 miles north and turn left for the visitors center. It can also be reached from US 422 and PA 23.

Stop in at the visitors center to see the exhibits and a short film. Most of this hike is on the paved Multi-use Trail, and walking shoes are preferable. Bicyclists and joggers are also permitted on the Multi-use Trail, so keep an eye out, particularly for the bicycles.

The Trail

This hike starts just beyond the auditorium and administration buildings. Head left and circle the visitors center. The trail continues along PA 23. In addition to dogwood and redbud, catalpa, sweet gum, and white pine grow here.

Cross County Line Road and climb gently. At 1.5 km pass a monument to patriots of African descent, then a side road to the site of General Hunting-don's quarters. Like most such buildings at Valley Forge, it is not open to the public.

At 1.9 km a path leads to the grave of a Lieutenant Waterman, the only identified grave of all the men who died that winter. Then you pass some reconstructed huts. They are dark and windowless, but sanitized—no dense, choking smoke issuing from the green wood burning in the chimneys, no groans or stench of men dying from "the bloody flux." Over 1000 huts were built to shelter the Continental army that winter, but they were not completed in time for the army's arrival on December 19; it was mid-January before all the men could be housed. Next, pass the headquarters of General Varum. There seems to have been no shortage of generals at Valley Forge. Today such a force would have only one.

Veer left to pass a statue of Friedrich von Steuben, a Prussian officer between jobs, not knowing a word of English but with a generous supply of

German and French curses, who came to Valley Forge in late February 1778. Unlike American officers, he worked directly with the enlisted men. Von Steuben taught by example and intensively trained a special group of 100 men who then returned to their units to train the rest of the troops. Because many units were using different training manuals, he wrote a new, uniform manual for the whole army. More than any other man, von Steuben is credited with turning a motley mix of soldiers into a disciplined fighting force at Valley Forge. The Grand Parade on which he trained his hand-picked group is to your left.

Turn left, away from PA 23, and at 2.9 km turn left again on the historic road trace. This road led north to a bridge over the Schuylkill River built that winter to bring in supplies. The road seems to have escaped much resurfacing since then.

Cross Gulph Road and bear left on the Multi-use Trail at 4.0 km. Next, turn left and circle Wayne's Woods to a picnic area with rest rooms. Continue past more huts, then circle the National Memorial Arch. (The arch is dilapidated and pieces of it keep falling off, so you can't go through it.) Soon, the Multi-use Trail parallels the Outer Line Defenses at the

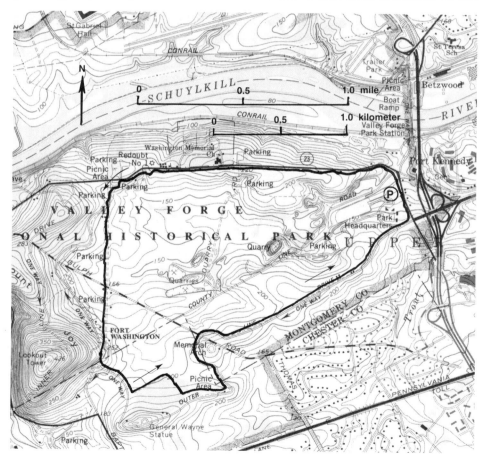

top of a hill. Half a dozen brigades manned this line. Pass more huts and redoubt 2, which anchored the left flank of the Outer Line. Then cross two roads and complete your hike of Valley Forge at the administration building.

Additional hiking opportunities in the area can be found on Mount Joy, west of Valley Creek and north of the Schuylkill River. However, these trails are difficult to integrate with this hike because of bridge crossings and missing trail sections.

20

Holtwood Recreation Area

Location: 15 miles south of Lancaster

Distance: 8.1 km (5.0 miles)

Time: 3¼ hours

Vertical rise: 250 meters (820 feet)

Highlights: Conestoga Trail, view, stream

Maps: USGS 7½' Holtwood; recreation area map

The Holtwood Recreation Area, near the Maryland border, is owned by Pennsylvania Power and Light (PP&L) and was developed as part of the Holtwood Dam hydroelectric project when PP&L acquired tracts of land on both sides of the Susquehanna River. The Kelly's Run–Pinnacle Trail System is within this land on the river's east side.

PP&L has designated much of this site as Kelly's Run Natural Area, which means it will remain protected in its natural state. The Kelly's Run–Pinnacle Trail System has been designated a National Recreation Trail by the US Department of the Interior.

As there is at least one stream crossing and a lot of rocks, you will want your boots for this hike.

How to Get There

The Holtwood Recreation Area is reached from PA 372. Turn north on Crystal Drive, 1.0 mile east of the Norman Wood Bridge over the Susquehanna. Then drive north 0.8 mile to the parking lot.

The Trail

Turn to your right and follow the edge of the woods until you see a post sign that says CONESTOGA TRAIL. Then head into the woods on a broad trail following blue (Kelly's Run Trail) and orange (Conestoga Trail) blazes. In a few steps you cross the yellow-blazed Oliver Patton Trail, named for the original farmer of this area.

The Conestoga Trail, built by the Lancaster Hiking Club, runs from the Horse Shoe Trail crossing at US 322 to the Mason-Dixon Trail at the Lock 12 (Susquehanna and Tide Water Canal) historic area. It's about 105 km long. The best parts are from PA 372 north along the Susquehanna to Pequea and then east to Martic Forge.

Back on the Kelly's Run Trail, you soon pass under a power line. The

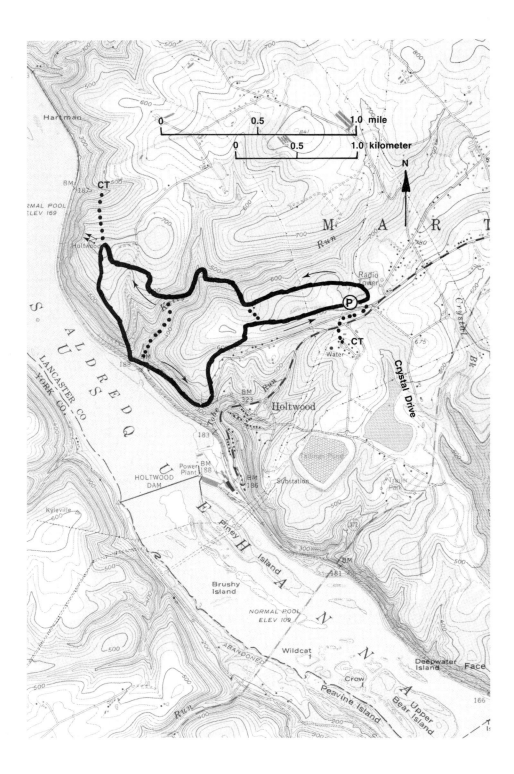

Holtwood Dam supplies power at times of peak demand; transmission lines spread out in many directions. Next, cross the other side of the Oliver Patton Trail. Pass under another power line.

At a junction with the red-blazed Loop Trail on your left, the Kelly's Run Trail descends steeply to the run itself. (You could use the Loop Trail to truncate this hike by connecting with the Kelly's Run Return Trail.)

At 1.8 km, there are cliffs of Wissahickon schist and the trail passes through rhododendrons. Cross Kelly's Run, then a side stream, and continue downstream.

Note that many of the hemlocks in this valley are dead or dying. This is due to the woolly adelgid, an aphid that sucks the juices from hemlock needles, weakening the trees. Some believe that hemlocks will go the way of the American chestnut at the turn of the last century, for the woolly adelgid has no natural enemies. *Tsuga canadensis* is Pennsylvania's state tree; it's scary to imagine our forests without these beautiful trees.

At 2.4 km continue ahead on the white-blazed Pinnacle Trail. (You have another opportunity to shorten this hike by bearing left here on the Kelly's Run Trail.) Climb on the Pinnacle Trail and turn left, crossing first an old road, then a telephone cable swath. Turn right on a fire road that is also blazed yellow.

Note an old stone wall as you climb: Somebody tried to farm this land. Pass a gate at the Pinnacle parking area and bear left to the overlook. There is a sweeping view across Lake Aldred and up to Otter Creek on the other side. Lake Aldred is formed by the Holtwood Dam. There are picnic tables and drinking water here in-season. "And when I asked the name of the river and heard it was called the Susquehanna; the beauty of the name seemed to be part and parcel of the beauty of the land . . ."—Robert Louis Stevenson.

To return, head back to the gate and bear right on the Fire Line Trail, blazed both yellow and orange. Soon you pass the other end of the stone wall you saw on your way up.

At 4.3 km, bear right on the Conestoga Trail and descend, passing a lookout ledge to your right. Jog right 30 meters on the telephone cable swath, and continue in the woods. Next, turn right on a woods road for 100 meters; then turn left on rough trail that descends the rocky spine of the ridge.

Turn right on the Kelly's Run Trail at 5.0 km, then left on a paved road closed to traffic. Cross Kelly's Run on the road bridge and climb to a gate at the edge of a road open to traffic.

Turn left and left again, passing another gate. Climb on a grassy road to the edge of a field, where you turn left. Then turn right and cross the field on a track.

You will reach a junction with the other end of the red-blazed loop trail at 7.2 km. Cross a power line and pass a pine plantation. Cross another power line to arrive at the gate at the corner of the parking lot.

Additional hiking opportunities here include the Pine Tree Trail from the Pinnacle Overlook, and the Oliver Patton Trail. Or you could follow the Conestoga Trail north along the rugged river hills to Pequea or Martic Forge.

Stone Bridge over Porter Run

21

Tyler State Park

Location: just west of Newtown

Distance: 8.7 km (5.4 miles)

Time: 2½ hours

Vertical rise: 110 meters (360 feet)

Highlights: a pleasant walk in the country

Maps: USGS 7½' Langhorne; park map

Tyler State Park in Bucks County (not to be confused with Tyler Arboretum in Delaware County) was purchased with Project 70 funds, then developed with funds from the Pennsylvania Land and Water Conservation and Recreation Act. There are a total of 38 km of trails in the park. Most are paved multiuse trails for bicyclists, walkers, joggers, hikers, and, in some places, equestrians. Neshaminy Creek divides the park into the eastern section, which is developed, and the western, where most of the trails are located. Since the Schofield Covered Bridge was destroyed by arson in 1991, the only link between east and west is a pedestrian causeway near the boathouse parking area.

Two low dams on Neshaminy Creek provide some slack water for boating. There is a youth hostel near the northern end of the park, and you may meet cars going to or from the hostel.

About 25 percent of the park is leased for agriculture; corn, winter wheat, hay, and soybeans are grown. After harvest, the cornfields are invaded by hundreds of Canada geese swooping down for fast food; some of the geese are permanent residents, but park officials hope that most are still migratory. There is no hunting at Tyler Park.

This hike is mostly on paved trails, so walking shoes are fine.

How to Get There

Tyler State Park is on PA 413 at its junction with Swamp Road. This part of PA 413 is the four-lane bypass just west of Newtown. The park can also be reached from exit 27 off the Pennsylvania Turnpike. Drive east on PA 332 from Willow Grove to Richboro, and continue to the park. PA 332 forms Tyler's southern boundary and intersects with PA 413 just east of the park.

There is a parking lot on No. 1 Lane (off PA 332) that you could use. This hike, however, uses the boathouse parking lot. From the main entrance on PA 413, follow Swamp Road for 0.4

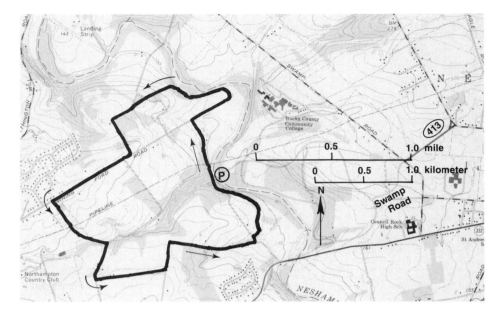

mile to a stop sign. Turn right on Main Park Road and drive 1.2 miles to the end, where you will find the boathouse parking lot.

The Trail

This circuit hike makes a grand tour of the western part of the park. Start by crossing the pedestrian causeway; the Neshaminy Weir Dam is just upstream. Then turn right on the Mill Dairy Trail, passing tulip trees and white oaks. At 600 meters you walk by a historic farm building. In the park, these houses are owned by the state but leased to private persons.

At 0.8 km, turn right on the Dairy Hill Trail. This and other major trail junctions are marked with signs. Red oak, shagbark hickory, sassafras, and hemlock trees can be seen along this trail. It returns to Neshaminy Creek, where you may hear the rattling call of the kingfisher. Note poison ivy vines climbing up trees along the trail. It's really a beautiful vine: The leaves turn red in the fall and it bears an abundance of white berries, eaten by birds.

At 2.5 km you reach a junction with the Covered Bridge Trail. There is a drinking fountain at this junction. Continue ahead on the White Pine Trail. (Yes, it really does have white pines.) Along the park boundary you pass a working farm.

Turn right at a junction with the Dairy Hill Trail at 3.3 km. The Dairy name figures in a number of trails because the Tylers, who owned this land before it became a park, operated a dairy farm here.

Next, pass a junction with the Hay Barn Grass Trail and continue to the park boundary, passing private homes. Turn left on the College Park Trail at 4.2 km. As usual, equestrian trails weave in and out of the hiker-biker trails.

Turn right on the No. 1 Lane Trail and cross a stone bridge. At another historic house you reach the end of a road. Cross a bridge and turn left on the Stable Mill Trail. As noted earlier, there is a parking lot ahead that can be reached from PA 332.

Pass the Gallery (Pennsylvania crafts), another parking lot, and a white stone house where the road is blocked to vehicles.

Osage orange is an abundant tree along this section. It produces bright green fruits that look like warty oranges but are of a very different consistency.

At 6.4 km there is a junction with the Natural Area Trail, which is different from the Nature Trail along Porter Run. Turn left on the Mill Dairy Trail at 7.3 km, cross a bridge, and bear right on the Woodfield Trail. This is a fitness trail, but the exercises are optional.

Turn right on the Mill Dairy Trail again, walking among some beech trees. Pass the other end of the Natural Area Trail. Cross a stone bridge over Porter Run, turn right, cross the pedestrian causeway, and return to your car.

22

Mill Creek

Location: 10 miles southeast of Reading

Distance: 10.9 km (6.8 miles)

Time: 4 hours

Vertical rise: 320 meters (1050 feet)

Highlights: large rocks, creek

Maps: USGS 7½' Elverson, Pottstown; park map

This hike explores the roadless eastern section of French Creek State Park. For over a century the Hopewell Iron Furnace produced iron from local ores and charcoal. The charcoal was itself produced from trees growing on the hills around French Creek. These hills were repeatedly denuded of trees, marginalizing the land. Then, during the Great Depression of the 1930s, the lands were purchased by the federal government. Today's forest shows how well the hills have recovered.

There are rocks and a lot of wet areas along the trail, so wear your hiking boots.

How to Get There

French Creek State Park can be reached from exit 22 off the Pennsylvania Turnpike: Follow PA 10 to Morgantown, then take PA 23 east to PA 345. The park is also accessible from exit 23: Follow PA 100 north to PA 23, then drive west on PA 23 to PA 345.

The trailhead is on PA 345 at its junction with Shed Road. This spot is 4.8 miles north of the junction with PA 23 and just 0.2 mile north of the east entrance to the park. Leave your car in a small area on the right, just beyond Shed Road. There is no sign at the trailhead.

The Trail

Cross Shed Road and head into the woods on the Mill Creek Trail, whose blazes are white with a red stripe across the middle. There are also green blazes here for the Lenape Trail, which also follows this part of the Mill Creek Trail.

Soon you bear right on a gated old road and climb gently. At 0.5 km, continue straight ahead on the Mill Creek Trail where the Lenape Trail diverges to the right. (You will return on the Lenape Trail.) Cross a power line and reach a junction where the Mill Creek Trail splits. Turn left on

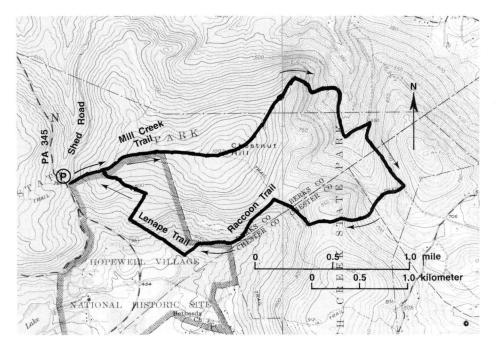

the trail and descend gently, passing a charcoal pit, to Millers Point at 2.9 km. Millers Point is a large rock formation. It is easily climbed, but there is no view. White oak, maple, and sassafras grow on the uplands.

In-season the ground hereabouts is covered with mayapples. Stay on the Mill Creek Trail as it turns right and descends, passing a spring. Then turn left at a junction with a blue-and-red-blazed trail. (You could truncate your hike by turning right at this junction.)

Continue descending to 3.5 km, where you turn right. There are some good-sized tulip trees here in Mill Creek Valley.

The French Creek Trail System east of PA 345 is heavily used by mountain bikes. On the uplands they produce minimal damage. The wet areas in Mill Creek Valley are another matter, however; here the bikes produce deep ruts and churn the wet spots into mud holes. It is difficult to pick your way around these stretches.

This section of the trail has some old white blazes in addition to the white ones with the red stripe.

At 4.2 km, cross the first part of Mill Creek. The trail continues among large boulders. Just after a junction with the red-blazed Raccoon Trail (which could be used to shorten this hike), cross the main part of Mill Creek.

Then turn sharply right at 4.6 km and climb gently on an old eroded road. (To the left, this old road leads out to Sycamore Road.) At 5.4 km, where the old road continues ahead, turn right on trail.

In-season you can find spring beauties and jack-in-the-pulpits along the trails. Cross the headwaters of Mill Creek and climb gently. Beech trees and black birch grow along this section.

After you reach the top of the hill, turn right onto the Mill Creek Trail at a junction with the red-and-yellow-blazed Buzzards Trail. (You could extend this hike by following the Buzzards Trail into the southeast part of French Creek Park.) Next, the red-blazed Raccoon Trail comes in from the right and merges with the Mill Creek Trail.

At 7.2 km, turn left on the Raccoon Trail to vary your return. Follow it downhill, reaching the boundary of the Hopewell Furnace National Historic Site. At 8.0 km an unblazed trail comes in from the left, past the ruins of a stone building. Cross under the power line again.

Turn right onto the green-blazed Lenape Trail at 8.5 km. You will come to a bridge over a small stream. To the right, a short unblazed trail leads to a spring that bubbles up out of the rocks; to the left you can see a field through the trees, with Williams Hill beyond. Continue on, passing a springhouse to the left and climbing steps made from creosoted utility poles. A century ago such springs provided settlers with much of their best water. Now they are all polluted.

The Lenape Trail switchbacks up the hill to 10.4 km, where you bear left again on the Mill Creek Trail. Retrace your steps to your car on PA 345.

French Creek State Park has nearly 50 km of trails. This hike—together with Hike 26—uses only 30 of them, so there are plenty of additional hiking opportunities at French Creek.

23

The Pinnacle

Location: 3 miles northeast of
Hamburg

Distance: 14.0 km (8.7 miles)

Time: 5 hours

Vertical rise: 315 meters (1030 feet)

Highlights: views, mountain stream

Map: USGS 7½' Hamburg

The Pinnacle is the most famous view
on the Appalachian Trail in Pennsylvania, and one of the best in the state.
A view from the Pinnacle is on the
cover of *Pennsylvania Hiking Trails*,
11th edition. This trail's usage level is
comparable to that of Hawk Falls,
making it one of the most heavily traveled in the state.

This hike has more than its fair share
of rocks, so wear your hiking boots.

How to Get There
Take exit 10 off I-78 at Hamburg. Follow Fourth Street south to a Uni-Mart
and Getty station. Turn sharply right
on Port Clinton Avenue and proceed
for 0.6 mile, passing under I-78. Turn
right on Mountain Avenue at a sign

for Blue Mountain Camp. Drive 2.8
miles (the road name changes to Mountain Road) and turn left on Reservoir
Road. In 0.4 mile you reach the parking area, just before a chain-link fence
at the Hamburg Reservoir. No overnight parking is permitted here.

The Trail
At the trailhead, a large NO TRESPASS-
ING sign proclaims the entire water
company area off-limits. Actually, the
company is far more generous and
does permit day hiking. Please read
the posted regulations and abide by
them so that this happy situation will
continue.

If the gate to the fenced-off area is
open, you can walk right through and
pick up the blue blazes beyond the
map board. If the gate is closed, use a
well-beaten path immediately to the
left of the fence.

Proceed up the blue-blazed gravel
road to a junction with the white-blazed
Appalachian Trail (AT). Turn right
and cross a bridge over Furnace Run;
then bear right again.

At 1.3 km, turn right onto another
old road at a trail junction. (The blue-
blazed side trail leads ahead to the
Windsor Furnace Shelter.) The old
road climbs gently, passing chestnut

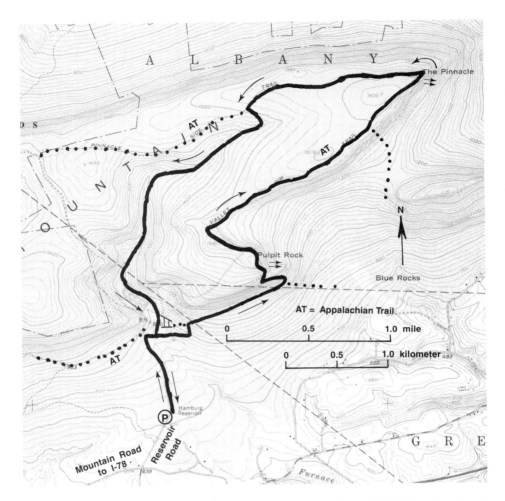

oak and sassafras trees, in addition to American chestnuts. Along this hike, note the many American chestnuts that continue to sprout from old roots, even after the chestnut blight killed the mature trees.

The serious climb starts at 2.5 km. At 3.0 km a blue-blazed side trail goes right to the Blue Rocks Campground. Stay on the old road until 3.5 km, where you turn right onto a rough trail with stone steps. The first of many patches of poison ivy is found here.

At 3.8 km you reach Pulpit Rock, with views to the east and south. A river of rocks, called Blue Rocks, is visible below. These views are just a sneak preview of those from the Pinnacle. Note the astronomical observatory to the left. It is difficult for even the smallest observatories to avoid light pollution, even in rural areas. In a city, you can't see even the brightest stars.

Follow the AT past an antenna site along the rocky edge of the ridge. At one point the trail passes through a crevasse. At 6.7 km there is a junction with a yellow-blazed trail on the right that also leads to the Blue Rocks Campground. Stay on the AT, which

View from Pinnacle

continues to be rough, rocky, and slow going.

At 7.3 km you reach a junction with a blue-blazed trail to the right that leads to the Pinnacle in 130 meters. Take this trail—but be careful, as there is a quite adequate drop to the rocks below. Views sweep east along heavily wooded Blue Mountain and then around to the south over farms, small towns, isolated hills, and the Cumberland Valley (the Great Valley of the Appalachians) to Furnace Hills on the horizon. Take your time savoring these views, but avoid the luxuriant poison ivy that grows here. The Blue Mountain Eagle Climbing Club maintains a trail register here.

When the flight of time urges you, return to the junction with the AT and keep right. The trail continues to be rocky until 8.0 km, where you reach the end of a jeep road. The AT follows this road past a couple of small ponds. Hemlocks and black gum trees grow here. Proceed to a large grassy area at 10.3 km, known as the heliport.

Turn sharply left on another jeep road partway across this clearing. This road makes for very easy hiking and you descend gently, passing a spring, then crossing Furnace Creek. (This is not Gold Spring, which is farther along and closer to the AT.) Black birch trees grow along the road, and the run has the expected stand of hemlocks.

There are a few blue blazes along the jeep road, but you don't really need them to find your way. Farther along, rhododendrons line the stream. This trail is quite a contrast to the AT between Pulpit Rocks and the Pinnacle.

At 12.4 km you reach the Hamburg Reservoir itself. Keep left, passing the dam. Continue ahead, ignoring a road to the left. At a junction with the AT, you close your loop by turning right, crossing Furnace Run, then turning left onto the blue-blazed road back to your car.

You could extend this hike about 1.5 km by following the AT "north" (toward Maine) to a woods road that descends Blue Mountain west of the reservoir. This route avoids Furnace Creek, however.

24

Wilderness Trail

Location: 4 miles northwest of Media	
Distance: 14.1 km (8.7 miles)	
Time: 5½ hours	
Vertical rise: 245 meters (800 feet)	
Highlights: Tyler Arboretum	
Maps: USGS 7½' Media; visitor's guide	

The plantings at the Tyler Arboretum were begun by Minshall and Jacob Painter, who set aside part of their land for the systematic planting of trees and shrubs. Only about 20 of the original trees planted in the mid-19th century survive, but they are of real size. Among these original Painter trees are a cedar of Lebanon that is over 4.5 meters in circumference and a giant, vintage-1856 sequoia. Even if you come back in 800 years, though, this one won't look like sequoias in the Sierras: This specimen has two trunks because a Christmas tree thief cut off its top in 1895.

This hike takes you on a grand tour of the 260-hectare arboretum. It is difficult to squeeze this long a trail into such a small area, so it has been folded and refolded to increase its length. There are seven blazed trails at Tyler, ranging in length from 2 km (the Dogwood and Pinetum Trails) on up to the 13.6 km Wilderness Trail. In addition to the blazed trails at Tyler, there are a host of unblazed trails and old roads. Admission to this private, not-for-profit educational institution is $3 per person. Spring, when the shrubs and wildflowers are in bloom, is the best time to visit.

How to Get There
The Tyler Arboretum is located just off PA 352 about 4 miles north of Media; or you can take PA 352 south from PA 3 for 5.1 miles. In either case, turn east onto Forge Road, then right onto Painter Road to the parking lot.

The Trail
From the bulletin board at the corner of the parking lot, make your way toward the barn that houses the bookstore and rest rooms. Keep to the left of the building and descend a flight of steps to the cedar of Lebanon. Avoid the branch that touches the ground and continue to a bridge over Rocky Run, which serves as the trailhead.

The Wilderness Trail is blazed white.

The sign at the loop junction indicates that these blazes are square, but they are in fact frequently rectangular and on their sides. Ignore all other-colored blazes. At the sign for the Wilderness Trail, take the left fork.

Along the way you will see azalea, rhododendron, dogwood, and lots of tulip trees. On the other hand, there is remarkably little poison ivy at Tyler. Turn right just beyond a fence at 1.2 km; a field to the left contains a dogwood. At 1.5 km turn left. A field of dogwood is to the right.

Cross Rocky Run at 2.2 km, then turn left and climb. Rocky Run has an abundance of skunk cabbage. Turn right, along the boundary between Ridley Creek Park and the Tyler Arboretum, at 2.6 km. There is a white pine plantation on the park side of the trail. Pass a trail leading into the state park.

At 3.0 km bear right, away from the boundary, on a recent relocation. Jog left at the next junction. At 3.3 km, the trail has recently been hacked through the brush. Just beyond there is a bridge over a stream; turn right on an old road and climb.

There is an inviting bench at 3.7 km. Next, descend and turn sharply left above Rocky Run. Turn right at 4.0 km, at a corner marked with double arrows as well as double blazes, and recross Rocky Run on stepping-stones. Climb the hill and, at 4.9 km, turn left where a field of dogwood lies ahead. Then turn left again at the corner of another field. There are ruins to the left of the trail at 5.4 km; turn sharply left and pass below them.

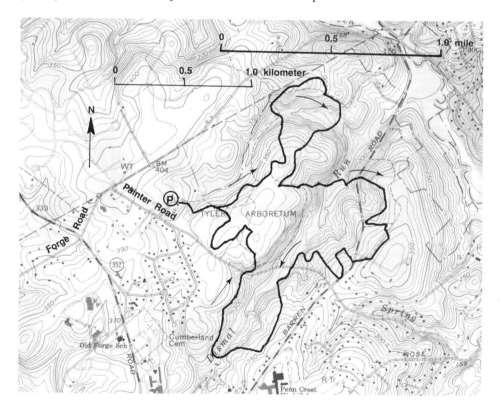

The Wilderness Trail

Cross a bridge over Dismal Run and pass through a small fish hatchery. Note that the road here is on top of an old dam. At the far side of the valley, cross an old millrace. At 5.8 km turn left off the road and pass through the floodplain of Dismal Run. Then turn left on an old road and climb to Barren Road at 6.4 km. Cross with care and enter the east woods.

There is much less of a footway here, and you must move carefully from blaze to blaze. At 7.3 km, the trail returns to Barren Road before turning sharply left. There is a woodlot management trail along this section.

Cross Barren Road again at 8.9 km, then turn *left* at a confusing spot (the arrow is intended for hikers going in the opposite direction). The trail reclimbs the hill before turning right near the junction of Painter and Barren Roads. At 9.9 km there is another confusing spot, where the white blazes bear to the right, then return to the old road. You could follow the blazes at this point, or just go straight ahead.

At 10.1 km cross Painter Road, then a stream, and climb to the edge of a field. Continue along the upper edge of this field, passing a bench under a cedar tree. The trail returns to Barren Road before turning right. Houses can be seen on adjacent private land along this section.

Cross Dismal Run on a log at 11.4 km. In high water, this could be interesting. Then turn left and proceed to 11.6 km, where you turn right. At 12.0 km, pass another ruin with two keystone arches; turn right again. Cross Painter Road for a second time at 12.5 km. At 12.7 km, turn right along the edge of an open area. Turn left into this open area at 12.8 km. Follow the blazes carefully, as there are very few of them. Turn left again at 13.0 km and follow trail past larches, then past the giant sequoia. Reenter the woods at 13.4 km and turn left among rhododendrons. Close the loop at 13.8 km, cross the bridge over Rocky Run, and retrace your steps to the parking lot.

There are six other blazed trails at Tyler but you have already covered many sections of them on the Wilderness Trail. There are also hiking opportunities at nearby Ridley Creek State Park; see Hike 16.

25

Delaware Canal

Location: 10 miles south of Easton

Distance: 17.3 km (10.8 miles)

Time: 4½ hours

Vertical rise: 15 meters (50 feet)

Highlights: National Heritage Trail

Maps: USGS 7½' Riegelsville, Frenchtown (NJ); park map

Following the success of the Erie Canal in 1825, Pennsylvania pursued a canal-building program in order to keep up with New York State. The Delaware Canal, 96 km long, was opened in 1832. Boats hauled coal, lumber, iron, and stone downriver, but they had trouble finding heavy cargoes for the return journey. Moving night and day, a canal boat took 2 days to traverse the canal from Easton to tidewater at Bristol, for an average of 2 km per hour. This is about half the rate at which you can walk the towpath.

Canals contained the seeds of their own destruction. First, they could operate only during the ice-free months. Trains had no such limitation. Second, canals had to be built along rivers to get the water they required. Rivers flood, and when they do they can damage or destroy a canal. Finally, canals were the first large-scale engineering projects in this country, and they trained a generation of engineers—who went on to build railroads.

Despite the odds against it, the Delaware Canal continued to operate until 1932. Thus, it survived more or less intact. Almost all of it still contains water, but the locks don't work anymore. The canal became a state park in 1940.

This is a long but easy (easy to follow and easy on your feet) hike on the canal's towpath. There is scarcely any change in elevation, and the footway is mowed grass and dirt. Save for the occasional tree root, you don't have to watch every step; you can look around. But do not stray off the towpath onto private land. Relations with adjacent owners are generally good; let's keep it that way. None of the park is open to hunting, but some may occur on private lands near the canal.

How to Get There

The linear structure of the canal dictates a car-shuttle hike. The canal is

Towpath and canal

paralleled by PA 32 and PA 611. The northern end of this hike is at Lock 21, which is 1.8 miles north of Kintnersville, at the junction of PA 212 with PA 611. Parking places along the canal are hard to find, but there are a modest number here. Leave one car here and head south on PA 611. In Kintnersville, turn left on PA 32 and drive 9.4 miles to Tinicum County Park. Turn right and make your way to the edge of the canal, about 0.4 mile, where there is a small parking lot.

The Trail
Head north along the canal. This particularly attractive section follows the base of the hills; the highway is some distance away. At 900 meters you pass several houses. Many people live right on the canal. Some of the houses are definitely upscale, but there are also trailer camps.

The first bridge you reach is the only covered bridge on the canal. It is at 2.2 km, just before Lock 18. There are a lot of other bridges over the canal: I counted 19, including the one at Lock 21.

There are a great many different trees along the canal. I found maple, osage orange, pin oak, catalpa, white pine, sycamore, locust, willow, and river birch. Trees that grow next to the towpath enjoy an abundance of water and may achieve impressive size.

On this hike I've also seen great blue herons, kingfishers, juncos, titmice, chickadees, and a broad-winged hawk. Bluebird houses at some spots mean that in summer you should look for this bird that carries the sky on his back. Along the more isolated sections of the towpath you may find deer and raccoon tracks in the mud.

In some places the hills on the far side of the canal become real cliffs. At 5.2 km you reach Lock 19 and the Delaware Canal State Park headquarters. There is intermediate parking at

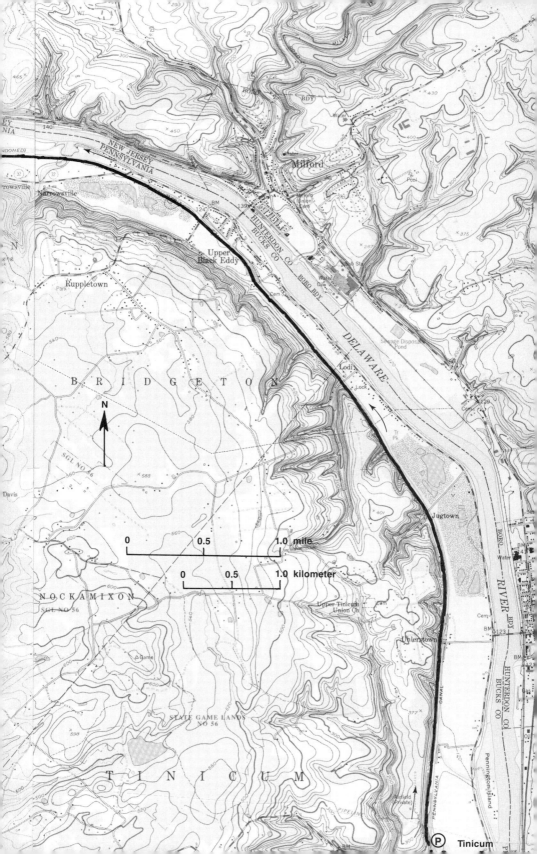

Lock 19. On occasion there are mileposts along the towpath, but many seem to be missing.

You will find the Country Store at 7.6 km. Here you can obtain deli sandwiches and baked goods, and there is a rest room for customers. Beyond, the Delaware River becomes visible briefly. At 8.5 km, PA 32 goes over the canal on a bridge next to the Manor House, an upscale restaurant.

At 11.5 km you can see PA 32 on one side, the Delaware on the other. Next, you pass the Indian Rock Inn. The cliffs tower in this area, and some people think they see the profile of a Native American in them. Don't spend too much time looking for it.

At 12.7 km, you pass the Gilbert generating plant on the New Jersey side of the river. Next, you come to Lock 20, which has some picnic tables and is alleged to have some parking along the highway.

After a riffle in the Delaware, you will cross—at 13.9 km—Gallows Run aqueduct. Traugers Farm Market is at 15.7 km. PA 611 is now on the other side of the canal. Finally, you reach Lock 21 and your car.

There is additional hiking along the canal both north and south of this section, but finding parking places is a problem. To the north there is parking at Locks 22 and 23, Wy-Hit-Tuk County Park, and the Hugh Moore Park and Canal Museum in Easton. (After your hike, this museum is worth a visit.) To the south there is parking at Erwinna, the Mountain Side Inn (abandoned) south of Point Pleasant, Lumberville (a pulloff), the Virginia Forest Recreation Area, New Hope (on the street), Chez Oddets (park property) south of New Hope, Bowmans Hill in Washington Crossing Historical Park ($1 fee), the junction of PA 532, and Yardley (on Black Road).

26

French Creek State Park

Location: 11 miles southeast of Reading

Distance: 18.5 km (11.5 miles)

Time: 6½ hours

Vertical rise: 353 meters (1160 feet)

Highlights: Horse Shoe Trail

Maps: USGS 7½' Elverson; park map

French Creek (2900 hectares), between Reading and Philadelphia, is one of the large state parks that were operated as demonstration national parks by the federal government during the Great Depression. Recreational facilities such as dams, roads, picnic areas, group camps, and tent camping areas were built by the Civilian Conservation Corps (CCC). Those who loved Franklin Roosevelt said that the CCC was the best thing he did for the country. Those who hated him said the CCC was the only good thing he did. Even today, many of our recreation areas stem from the CCC.

The program also saved a genera-tion of young men from becoming homeless drifters, when they finished school only to find no jobs available. The CCC offered a little money and hearty meals to young men, physical work in the out-of-doors, and military discipline. The 3 million who were trained under this system became a large, albeit unorganized, reserve. Virtually all the men who had been in the CCC served in World War II; in December 1941, many camps marched straight off to war.

The federal government bought up marginal areas such as French Creek during the Great Depression, giving the impoverished residents enough money to start over somewhere else with better chances. The land around French Creek had been logged repeat-edly to make charcoal for the Hopewell Iron Furnace, which operated from 1771 to 1883. (Hopewell iron was used to make cannons during the Ameri-can Revolution.) In 1946 the park was turned over to the state, with the excep-tion of a core area that the National Park Service retained as Hopewell Furnace National Historic Site.

This boot-busting hike makes a grand tour of the western part of the park. It is long, but you will have many opportunities to truncate it via other

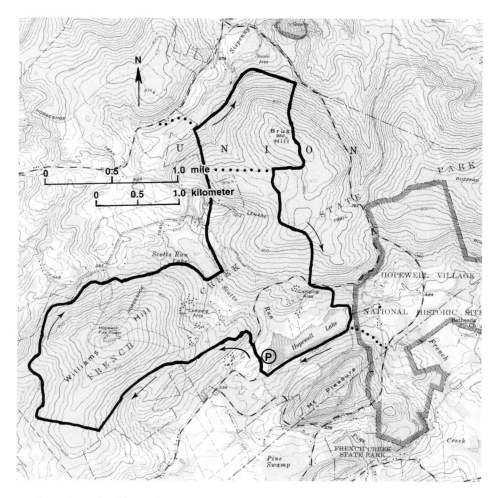

trails and roads. Given the many rocks and wet places, as well as the length of this hike, wear your boots.

How to Get There

French Creek can be reached from exit 22 off the Pennsylvania Turnpike. At the second traffic light in Morgantown, turn east onto PA 23 through Elverson. Then turn north onto PA 345 at Warwick. After 2.5 miles, turn left into the park at its south entrance. After 1.1 miles turn right onto Park Road at a stop sign. Proceed 0.5 mile past the park office to the Hopewell

Lake Boat Launch parking lot.

The park can also be reached from the north by following PA 345 south from just east of Birdsboro. Turn right on Park Road and proceed west to the Hopewell Lake Boat Launch.

The Trail

To start the hike, make your way to the parking lot entrance, turn right, and pick up the blue-blazed Boone Trail. Cross Park Road and head into the woods, climbing a low hill. Instead of the original chestnut forests, the hills are now covered with red, white, and chestnut oaks, as well as maple and tulip trees.

Turn left on the yellow-blazed Horse Shoe Trail at 0.7 km. The blue blazes also continue; sometimes they are on the same tree. The Horse Shoe Trail is virtually unique in the East, as it was built for both equestrians and hikers. Today it faces very serious problems arising from the lack of a continuous corridor of public land.

Next, bear left on the Horse Shoe Trail where the Boone Trail diverges right. At 1.6 km the white-blazed Turtle Trail comes in from your right. The Horse Shoe Trail has been relocated here to avoid going over Williams Hill, where horses produced severe erosion on both sides. All the trails at French Creek are multiuse—bicycles, horses, and hikers—and appear to be heavily traveled, although there are usually some chainsaw blowdowns. Now the trail is marked with both yellow blazes and white blazes.

There is a junction with a red-blazed trail at 4.7 km. Next, the Turtle Trail passes along the park boundary; you can see several houses on the adjacent private land. You will cross paved Fire Tower Road at 6.5 km. It is gated off to traffic, but there is trailhead parking just beyond the gate to your left.

The blue-and-white-blazed Boone Trail comes in from your right at 6.7 km. Continue on the yellow-blazed Horse Shoe Trail. Next, the Boone Trail diverges left and you pass the ruins of a trailside shelter to your right. Shelters are an idea whose time has gone; they date from the days of heavy canvas tents, and today's lightweight nylon tents have made them obsolete.

Soon you can see Scotts Run Lake ahead through the trees. Turn left and cross the dam rather than following the Horse Shoe Trail, which goes below the dam.

Pick up the Horse Shoe Trail again at the parking lot on the far side of the dam. Follow it into the woods and through a white pine plantation to paved Scotts Run Road at 8.7 km. Ahead, the Horse Shoe Trail continues on the gated road leading to the group tenting area.

Proceed up the gated road, passing a field and then rest rooms. Cross the blue-blazed Boone Trail on a crossroad, then bear left on trail. The Horse Shoe Trail climbs a hill that shows signs of erosion. A bulldozer was being used to make water bars during my last hike here.

At the top of the hill, pass private land to your left; the orange-blazed trail joins from your right. Continue down the north side and pass a purple-blazed trail to your right. At 10.0 km turn right on the orange-marked trail, leaving the yellow-blazed Horse Shoe Trail.

Just before the Six Penny Area, pass a spring. There used to be a lake at Six Penny but it was drained years ago, and only a meadow remains. The trail passes the ruins of a building burned in spring 1995 by arsonists. Beyond, pick up the Six Penny Trail on a road and pass another junction with the purple-blazed trail. Just beyond the vandalized remains of an outhouse, turn sharply right on trail and climb. There are scattered giant mountain laurels along the trail. The traffic noise is from PA 345.

Turn right along an eroded road at 11.9 km and climb steadily up the side of Brush Hill. The trail has mostly been relocated to keep it out of the old road. Partway up, you pass a charcoal hearth to your right; this was once a charcoal road.

Just after reaching the top of the hill, bear left at the edge of an unpaved road. Then turn sharply right at a junction of unblazed trails and cross the unpaved road.

Just 300 meters beyond is a critical turn to your left. (If you miss this turn, you will return to the Horse Shoe Trail on the top of the hill.) This nameless trail is marked with orange blazes that have a green stripe across the middle. Next, cross an old woods road and circle the campground that you can see to your left. Jog left on the Boone Trail and in 50 meters the green-blazed Lenape Trail joins from your right.

The Boone and Lenape Trails diverge at 15.2 km. Turn right on the blue blazes. Then jog right, walk 60 meters on a paved road, and continue on the Boone Trail. Ignore a trail blazed with white circles directly ahead.

At 15.8 km, cross paved Park Road and turn left. The Boone Trail converges with this road and returns briefly to it before turning right and crossing the yellow-blazed Horse Shoe Trail. Next, turn left along the shore of Hopewell Lake. At the corner of the dam, meet the Horse Shoe Trail and turn right, passing below the dam and crossing the outlet. At the far end of the dam, the Horse Shoe Trail diverges to your left; you bear right on the Boone Trail along the lakeshore. Pass through a picnic area and circle the swimming pool.

At 18.2 km you emerge briefly on a paved road and turn right, crossing a bridge over an inlet to the lake. Then bear left, avoiding an unmarked trail along the shore, and emerge at the corner of a parking lot. Turn right, pass between the posts of a vehicle barrier, and close the loop at the Hopewell Lake Boat Launch.

There is an abundance of additional hiking at French Creek. Hike 22 explores the less developed section of the park east of PA 345.

27

Blue Marsh Lake

Location: 6 miles northwest of Reading

Distance: 22.5 km (14.0 miles)

Time: 7½ hours

Vertical rise: 385 meters (1260 feet)

Highlights: rolling terrain, lake

Maps: USGS 7½' Bernville, Sinking Spring; hiking trails map

Blue Marsh Lake backs up behind a flood-control dam on Tulpehocken Creek, about 10 km northwest of Reading. The dam was completed in 1979 by the US Army Corps of Engineers. Hiking is only one of the recreational opportunities developed at Blue Marsh Lake. Most of the recreation here is water-centered: fishing, boating, and swimming. Elsewhere, crops are grown on Corps of Engineers land, in part to attract wildlife for in-season hunting.

Besides some short interpretive trails, a major hiking trail has been created that permits you to encircle the lake, a distance of over 30 km. This hike uses the Blue Marsh Trail on the southwestern side of the lake— the side that is not as well developed with beaches, boat launches, and picnic areas.

This is a multiuse trail, with mountain bikers and horses sharing your path. Bikers should give way to hikers, who in turn should give way to horses. (Horses are temperamental creatures and may toss their riders off.) The trail is also open to in-season hunting.

How to Get There

This hike requires a car shuttle. To reach Blue Marsh Lake from US 222 in Reading, turn onto PA 183 and drive northwest for 5.8 miles. Turn left onto Plum Creek Road at a sign for Blue Marsh Lake and drive south for 2.1 miles. Turn right toward the Stilling Basin and leave one car in the lot there. In your other car, drive back to PA 183, turn left, and drive 2.8 miles. Then turn left onto Church Road (also known as SR 3006; there is a sign for Clover Hill Winery) and cross the bridge over the lake. Park at the trailhead on the left side of the road. Be sure to get your car completely off the road.

The Trail

The Blue Marsh Trail is marked with carsonite posts that display the logo of a hiker along with a directional

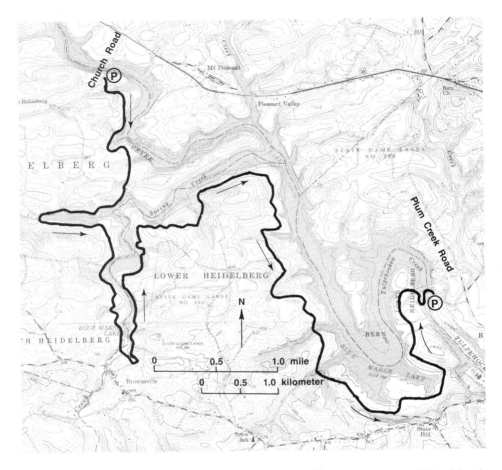

arrow, but it is easy to follow due to the heavy use it receives. Head down the trail, cross a stream, and bear left on an old paved road. Much of the Blue Marsh Trail is on old roads, some of them paved like this one. Then turn right onto a dirt road and climb, passing the mile-15 carsonite post. (The distances on the carsonite posts are greater than distances on the hiking trail map, which in turn are greater than my measurements.) Emerge into some fields at the top of the hill. The blue diamonds found here mark a side loop trail, as do the white diamonds farther along.

At 1.0 km, turn right and cross a bridge. Then pass an arm of Blue Marsh Lake. Note a small waterfall left of the trail farther on. There is a considerable amount of poison ivy along the trail. Turn right on a dirt road, then left on a paved road at 2.8 km; this is Skinners Road. Note the abandoned house to your left. Pass a barricade and, where the road dips into the lake, turn right.

The trail passes a stand of white pines and milepost 13. At 3.9 km, cross a bridge and bear right on paved Peacock Road. Turn left at the barricade and cross a bridge at 4.2 km. This is a possible intermediate access point; see the trail map for roads to reach it.

Bridge over Crane Creek

Pass along an arm of Blue Marsh Lake with fields to your right. Then turn and climb to the top of the hill among fields. (Only about a quarter of the land at Blue Marsh is wooded.) You will reach the end of Lamms Road at 5.5 km. This is the last practical access until the State Hill Boat Launch. Cross a stream on a board, then pass some stone walls among spruce trees.

Next, cross a long bridge perched on stone-filled wire baskets called gabions. This is Crane Creek. Continue along the edge of Reifsnyder Field to a bridge over Spring Creek at 6.9 km. Then turn left on a road and start back up this long arm of the lake. Keep going on the road, past a paved road to the right to Sleepy Hollow at 8.5 km. Here you turn right on trail, soon crossing a pipeline and milepost 9.

Cross Sterners Hill Road at 9.2 km and bear right on a gravel road. At 9.7 km, turn right at an unmarked corner and continue along the edge of a field. You will walk through a stand of hemlocks and reach four catalpa trees at 11.1 km; these must mark a former homestead. Pass some sickly-looking hemlocks and milepost 7.

Next, bear right on trail and walk directly along the lakeshore. Turn left on trail, cross a bridge, and switchback up a hill. Follow the edge of the next field to another crossing of Sterners Hill Road, at 14.8 km. Climb along the edge of a spruce plantation, then turn left to a view of the Dry Brooks Day-Use Area on the far side of the lake.

At 16.6 km, cross Dry Roads Farm bridge and pass milepost 4. Climb through jack pines. Then cross a bridge and bear left on paved Blue Marsh Road at 18.0 km. Pass the end of the Squirrel Run Nature Trail and a bench. Continue over a rise to the parking lot for the State Hill boat ramp at 18.4 km. Cross the upper end of the parking lot and turn right on the trail to Stilling Basin. Almost immediately, turn left onto a gravel road at 19.3 km. Then bear left again on a gravel road, passing milepost 2. Walk under a pole line where spruces are growing along this old dirt road.

At 20.4 km, cross an earthen berm that keeps floodwaters from overflowing when the dam is full. (You will want to visit Blue Marsh Lake between floods, as parts of this trail could otherwise be under water.) Beyond the berm bear left, then right on a paved road. Turn right on a dirt road at 21.2 km and cross the spillway, some 200 meters wide. Note the rock outcrops; these show that the spillway was cut into bedrock so that it wouldn't erode if the dam were to overflow here. You can see the State Hill Boat Launch across the lake.

At 21.9 km, pass the end of the dam (keep off) and continue on trail. Descend, but please don't cut off the switchback. Turn sharply left at the bottom and cross the outlet to reach the parking lot.

THE POCONOS

Hawk Falls

28

Hawk Falls

Location: Hickory Run State Park, near the junction of I-80 and PA 9

Distance: 4.8 km (3.0 miles)

Time: 2¼ hours

Vertical rise: 135 meters (440 feet)

Highlights: cascades and waterfalls

Maps: USGS 7½' Blakesley, Hickory Run; park map

Hickory Run State Park, at the western edge of the Poconos, is the setting for this short but challenging circuit hike. The challenge is to your pathfinding skills; you must follow a faint trail for 1.6 km along Mud Run. This trail was blazed at one time but has been neglected, and the blazes are now difficult to find and follow. In places it is overgrown with rhododendrons.

Despite its name, Mud Run is a beautifully clear stream attracting trout anglers (fly-fishing only) and kayakers (lots of drops). Mud Run flows through banks of rhododendrons on its way to the Lehigh River.

In addition, there is a bridgeless crossing of Hawk Run. When the water level is high enough for the falls to be impressive, the crossing gets interesting. There are stepping-stones, but they may be under water. Foot-logs appear during the summer, but they are later swept away by winter floods.

Wear your boots for this short hike; they will be useful for crossing Hawk Run. Carry sneakers if you don't want to get your boots wet. The stream bottom is very rocky, and you should not attempt to cross with bare feet.

Bicycles are prohibited on all trails at Hickory Run State Park.

How to Get There
Take exit 41 off I-80 and turn east on PA 534. Drive through Hickory Run State Park for 9.8 miles; just after you pass under the Pennsylvania Turnpike, park on the right. This is the trailhead for Hawk Falls.

The Trail
Start your hike by crossing the highway and heading east. Walk on the left, facing traffic; the shoulder is wider on this side, and you can see oncoming vehicles. After 600 meters turn right, crossing PA 534 to the organized group camping area. This is the Orchard Trail, although there isn't any sign. Pass a parking lot on the

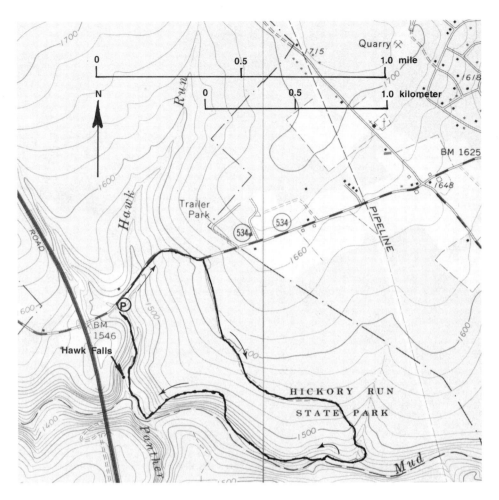

left, which is an alternative trailhead and could be used for a car shuttle if you prefer not to walk on PA 534.

Follow the road through the group camping area. The trees here are mixed hardwoods—beech, maple, and oak. There is another parking area at the end of the road just before a steel gate.

Beyond the gate, the road becomes grassy and rhododendrons grow along it. Watch for tiny red blazes, 2.5-by-7.5 cm in size. They are old and faded but all you have to follow along Mud Run. Double blazes are used to mark turns. These are definitely low-impact blazes.

Cross a stream, turn right at a small clearing, and cross the stream again on rocks. Reach Mud Run at 2.4 km and head downstream for 150 meters. Then turn right and climb the bank. Turn left—ignoring a red arrow pointing the other way!

There are occasional traces of footway as you move along, and they really help. But in some places the rhododendrons have closed in across the trail, and you must push through to find the next blaze.

By 2.8 km the trail returns to stream level, only to climb the bank again.

This is alleged to be an anglers' trail, but if so, it's the only one I've seen that is blazed and this long; anglers' trails usually go only as far as the first spot the fish are biting. Note the spruce trees growing along the trail.

At 3.1 km you are back to the stream for some nice cascades. This is one of the drops that attract kayakers. The trail crosses ledges of bare rock, then climbs very steeply away from Mud Run. At the top of the slope, turn left along the edge. Black cherry is one of the hardwoods growing here. The footway continues to twist and turn. Turn left at 3.9 km, then right again along the edge. Turn right on the Hawk Falls Trail at 4.1 km. You soon reach a wide side trail to Hawk Falls itself.

After you've seen the falls, return to the trail and the crossing of Hawk Run. The stepping-stones are fairly stable, even when they are under water. A stick of some sort is very useful for keeping your balance on them.

Beyond Hawk Run continue to PA 534; turn right to return to your car.

Other hiking opportunities abound at Hickory Run. The Boulder Field Trail, Hike 38, is on the other side of the highway; the Skyline Trail, Hike 29, is back near the park office. Hike 45 is longer and uses the Fourth Run, Gamewire, and Sand Spring Trails.

Hickory Run

29

Skyline Trail

Location: Hickory Run State Park, near the junction of I-80 and PA 9

Distance: 7.8 km (4.9 miles)

Time: 2¾ hours

Vertical rise: 215 meters (700 feet)

Highlights: mountain stream

Maps: USGS 7½' Hickory Run; park map

Hickory Run State Park, in the western part of the Poconos, is the setting for this hike. This large state park contains a wealth of hiking trails, ranging in length from 400 meters to 10 km, for a total of 60 km. It is not easy to keep up with the maintenance of such a system. In general, the trails here have signs at junctions but are unmarked or poorly blazed. Hikers are relatively invisible park users. They are out on the trails, not at the campground, swimming beach, or picnic area. This contributes to the low priority of trail maintenance. You'll see an example of a trail maintenance problem on this hike.

In general, trails at Hickory Run

do not have bridges, and you may have to rock-hop, walk on logs, or just wade across streams. It wouldn't hurt to carry a dry pair of socks in your pack. The stream bottoms are rocky and unkind to bare feet. This hike has two bridgeless crossings of Hickory Run, so you will want your boots.

How to Get There

This hike is in the western part of Hickory Run Park between PA 534 and the Lehigh River. To reach the park, take exit 41 from I-80 and drive east on PA 534 for 5.2 miles. Park on the right side of PA 534 between the HICKORY RUN TRAIL sign and the bridge over Hickory Run. If you reach the park office, you've gone 0.2 mile too far.

The Trail

To start, follow the highway back to the Hickory Run Trail. There is a well-beaten path outside the guide rail. Use it. Then bear left on the Hickory Run Trail and follow it through a meadow with old apple trees. Yellow birches also grow here. Farther on there are red oaks.

At 1.1 km, turn right on the Skyline Trail and climb the switchbacks up the side of the valley. This is a real trail, not an old road, and it is marked

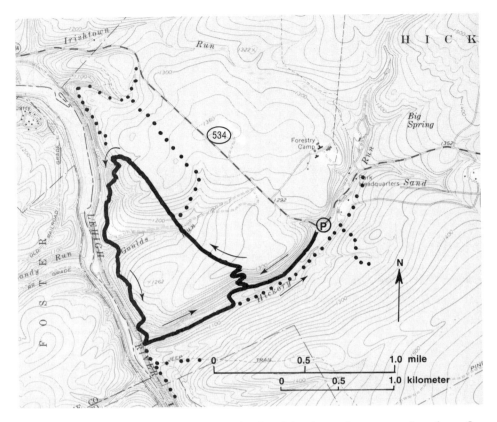

with occasional blue diamonds nailed to the trees. There are six switchbacks to the top of the hill.

At the crest the trail goes straight ahead, away from the edge. On my latest trip, though, the trail was blocked by the top of a maple tree that had blown down. The trail is rather faint at this point and you need all the help you can get to follow it. Instead of cutting through the top of the tree, the trail maintainer has taken out a section of the trunk off to the right—creating the impression that the trail goes in that direction. Detour around the blowdown and find the footway on the far side. Once you find the footway it is easy to follow. Soon there is a blue paint blaze. The blazing is certainly inadequate to follow this trail,

but it's nice to have occasional confirmation that you are still on it.

Next, you pass through an upland meadow with a sparse growth of birch trees. Then cross a stream and reach a junction of two versions of the Skyline Trail at 2.3 km. You could extend your hike by taking the right-hand version, which intersects the Fire Lane Trail farther to the north than this hike does.

Continue ahead at this junction through the upland meadow. Note the ground pine and ground cedar along the way. Then cross a woods road followed by an intermittent stream.

At 3.4 km, turn left on the Fire Lane Trail. (The extended version of this hike reenters here.) Then cross the same stream. There is a consider-able amount of up and down along the Fire Lane. Pass an old apple tree and reach the top of the first hill. Ignore a woods road that enters from your left. There is a meadow to your right with occasional views of the Lehigh River below. Note the blue-bird houses in the meadow.

Cross another stream and climb again. At 5.4 km, cross Hickory Run as best you can, then turn left on the Hickory Run Trail. This is a beautiful old road grade through hemlocks and rhododendrons.

Next, you reach a junction with the Sand Spring Trail. You could avoid recrossing Hickory Run by following the Sand Spring Trail to a junction with a short trail leading to the park office. You would then have to turn left on PA 534 to return to your car.

This hike instead turns left and recrosses Hickory Run. Shortly, you reach the junction with the Skyline Trail. Retrace your steps on the Hickory Run Trail to PA 534 and your car.

There are additional hikes in Hickory Run State Park on the Boul-der Field Trail (Hike 38), as well as around Hawk Falls (Hike 28), and Fourth Run (Hike 45).

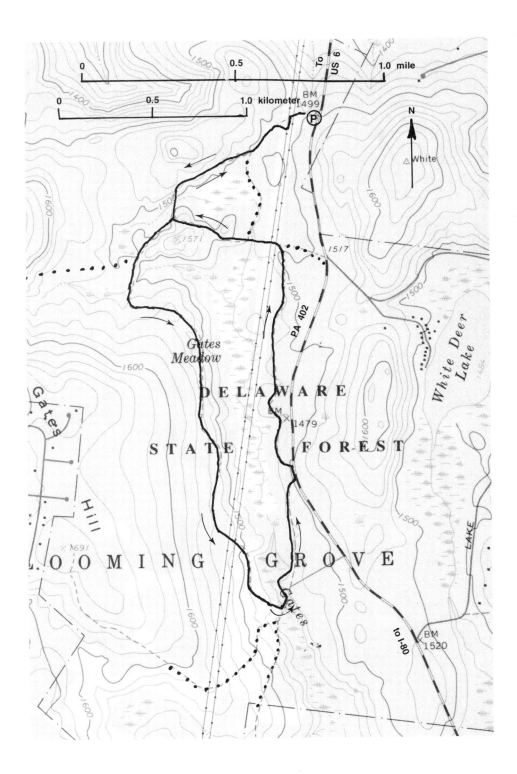

30

Blooming Grove Trail

Location: north of exit 8 off I-84

Distance: 7.9 km (4.9 miles)

Time: 3 hours

Vertical rise: 90 meters (300 feet)

Highlights: stream, wildflowers

Maps: USGS 7½' Hawley; forestry map

The Blooming Grove Trail is located in Delaware State Forest on PA 402 between I-84 and US 6. It consists of a Red Loop and a longer Blue Loop connected by the White Deer Trail. It was built by the 4-H Club of Pike County in 1975, in cooperation with the Bureau of Forestry. Since being reopened by Keystone Trails Association volunteers in April 1993, the trails are now maintained by volunteers from the Pocono Outdoor Club.

This hike is on an often rocky and sometimes wet trail, so wear your hiking boots. The pathway is almost flat but leads through surprisingly varied terrain.

How to Get There
Take exit 8 off I-84 and head north on PA 402 for 3.9 miles. There is a large parking lot, marked with a sign, on the west side of the highway. This parking area is about 1 mile south of US 6.

The Trail
The Blooming Grove Trail System is bisected by a double power line. To start the hike, head down the gated dirt road from the parking lot along this line and turn right to a map board at the edge of the woods. The red blazes start here. Bear right at a junction of red-marked trails at 230 meters. Soon you can see Blue Heron Swamp to the left. Next, cross a stream on logs. Look for fiddlehead ferns here in spring.

Turn right on the white-blazed White Deer Trail at 1.0 km. This junction is marked with a trail register. So far the route has been through mixed hardwoods—mostly black birches and oaks. Spring wildflowers along the trail are violets, fringed polygalas, and coneflowers.

At 1.3 km, turn left on the blue-blazed Gates Meadow Loop. Cross a stream on rocks and pass some vernal ponds. Look for tiny hop toads along

Gates Meadow Run

this section. The trail then enters white pines. Bracken grows here, along with highbush blueberries and mayapples.

Cross another stream. Shadbush are found here, and many small ones can be seen on the forest floor. Shadbush flowers in early spring, when the shad used to swim up the rivers to spawn— hence the name. Dams and pollution have now all but eliminated this annual migration.

Walk under the power line at 3.2 km. Cross a wet area on stepping-stones, then bear right along Gates Meadow Run. This area is particularly attractive, with an open stand of hemlocks along the stream. Enter a meadow with some spruce and turn left on a grassy road. Cross the run on a culvert. The water looks as if someone has made tea with it; this is due to iron tannate from the swamps and bogs that are drained by the run.

Turn left into the hemlocks and move upstream along the same run; turn right at 4.2 km. In low water you might be able to cross the run at this point, thus avoiding a downstream detour to the culvert.

Next, turn left on the grassy road. In mid-May the road is an azure carpet of bluets. Pass a clearing and turn left on another grassy road next to PA 402.

Keep left through a wet area at 5.0 km, followed by the big climb of the day—about 40 meters long. Turn right on trail at 5.2 km. There is a view of Gates Meadow Run to your left. Note the sheep laurel growing along the trail; it is smaller than mountain laurel but blooms at about the same time in June. Cross another wet area and jog left on a jeep road. There are a lot of black spruces growing along this section. Then enter hardwoods again.

Turn left on the white-blazed White Deer Trail at 6.3 km. In spring, look for painted trilliums. Cross the power-line swath and look for wild strawberries. After entering the woods you could find an obscure junction with a shortcut on a red-blazed trail to the right; this hike continues on the white blazes, however. Cross the outlet from Blue Heron Swamp on stones, and climb briefly.

Turn right on the red-blazed trail at the trail register and retrace your steps to your car.

Additional hiking opportunities can be found on the Thunder Swamp Trail (Hike 43) and at Promised Land State Park (Hike 42) and the Bruce Lake Natural Area (Hike 40). For a free trail map of the Blooming Grove Trail, write to Delaware State Forest, PO Box 150, Stroudsburg, PA 18360; or call 717-424-3001.

31

Bradys Lake

Location: 10 miles west of Pocono Summit

Distance: 7.9 km (4.9 miles)

Time: 2¼ hours

Vertical rise: 45 meters (140 feet)

Highlights: lake and swamp

Maps: USGS 7½' Thornhurst; SGL 127 map

State Game Lands (SGL) 127 in the Poconos was part of the Tobyhanna Military Reservation, acquired from the federal government in 1949. Other sections became Gouldsboro and Tobyhanna State Parks, but most of the reservation went to the Game Commission. Bradys Lake was built for ice production probably about 1892, when the Wilkes-Barre and Eastern Railroad was built.

This is a short circuit hike in a large, wild area of swamps and low hills. If the weather has been dry, walking shoes should be adequate on the excellent footway; there can be wet areas, however, particularly in cuts along the abandoned Wilkes-Barre and Eastern railroad grade.

How to Get There

From the traffic light at the intersection of PA 115 and PA 940 in Blakeslee, take PA 940 east for 5.0 miles. From the intersection of PA 423 and PA 940, take PA 940 west for 2.7 miles. Look for a junction with a mostly paved road; a small sign at this junction reads BRADYS LAKE PA FISH COMMISSION. Drive north on this road for 3.4 miles. The trailhead is at the dam forming Bradys Lake, and has ample parking.

The Trail

Follow the gated, paved road along the crest of the dam, crossing a bridge over the outlet. There are repeated views far down Bradys Lake. Its size reminds me of the large lakes in the Quetico-Superior wilderness along the Minnesota-Ontario border.

At the far end of the dam, the pavement ends and you turn right on a grassy road through a plantation of spruce and red pine. Surely this forest is as dark as any fairy-tale forest. At 0.9 km, bear right at a junction of old roads. You will return on the road from the left.

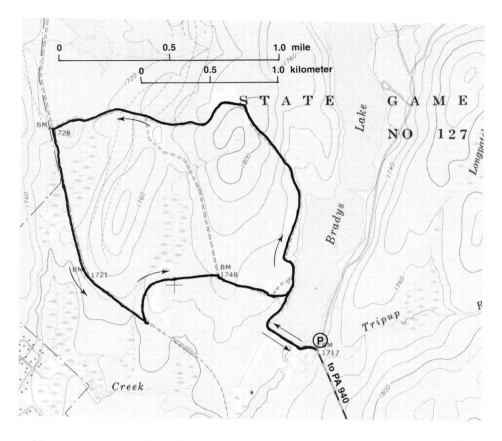

Next, cross a meadow. Here wild-flowers bloom far into the summer and fall. They are not confined to the brief period before the trees leaf out, as hardwood-forest-dwelling flowers are. The most abundant hardwoods are beech, maple, black cherry, and birch. Soon you enter a second meadow and walk left along its edge, passing old apple trees. Reach a third meadow and follow along its right side. At 3.2 km, you pass a junction with another road, which enters from the left. What appears to be red spruce grows along this section, and at 3.6 km you pass a large white pine.

Turn left on the old Wilkes-Barre and Eastern railroad grade at 4.0 km

(the same railroad as you will find at Big Pocono State Park). Note the cross-ties still in place. There is private land just ahead and the old road grade is blocked with a steel gate.

The old railroad crosses a swamp. In June turtles come up out of the swamp and lay their eggs in the rail-road ballast. The eggs are then dug up and eaten by opportunistic preda-tors, probably raccoons.

At 5.1 km you pass a benchmark on the right that lists the elevation as 1721 feet. Cross a stream and turn left on a railroad spur at 5.6 km. (If you miss this critical turn, there aren't any obvious landmarks until the game lands boundary, about 4 km farther south.) Avoid a road to the right just after this turn. Cross another meadow to reach a junction at 6.4 km. This appears to be the end of the spur, which was probably used to ship ice from Bradys Lake.

Turn right and follow an old road past a meadow fringed by aspens. Then bear left. Close the loop at 7.0 km; bear right and retrace your steps past the evergreen plantation and over the dam. Look for a beaver house in the ponds below the dam. The benchmark at the end of the dam is only 4 feet lower than the one on the railroad.

You could extend this hike by turning right when you reach the Wilkes-Barre and Eastern railroad and following it north for about 3 km, to the game lands boundary. Then return and complete the loop.

Two additional hikes in SGL 127, Artillery Ridge and Warnertown Falls, are described in *Pennsylvania Hiking Trails,* 11th edition. Warnertown Falls is a circuit hike, but it involves a bridgeless crossing of Tobyhanna Creek.

32

Mount Minsi

Location: in Delaware Water Gap

Distance: 7.9 km (4.9 miles)

Time: 3 hours

Vertical rise: 310 meters (1020 feet)

Highlights: views

Map: USGS 7½' Stroudsburg

Mount Minsi is on the Pennsylvania side of the Delaware Water Gap. It is not as imposing as Mount Tammany in New Jersey, but it makes a better hike. This section of Kittatinny Mountain is part of the Delaware Water Gap National Recreation Area. The recreation area was to be centered on the Tocks Island Dam, but that would have flooded the valley up to New York State. Other plans were for a scenic highway that would have destroyed the Appalachian Trail (AT) between Tott's Gap and the Delaware. Protests, some led by Supreme Court Justice William O. Douglas, halted these plans. The national recreation area now protects the free-flowing Delaware for us to enjoy.

Mount Minsi is part of the Shawan-gunk formation, containing coarse-grained sandstones and conglomerates of Silurian age (about 400 million years old). Farther west, parts of this formation are known as the Tuscarora sandstone; they extend to North Fork Mountain in West Virginia. To the north, the formation extends to the Shawangunk Mountains in New York State.

This is a circuit hike using the Appalachian Trail and the Mount Minsi fire road. Wear your hiking boots, as the AT is notoriously rough and rocky. Pennsylvania has the rockiest footway of all the 14 states on the AT and the rocks have turned many an ankle, including one of mine.

Northbound through-hikers should reach the Delaware in mid- to late June. Given the steep slopes here, you may have an opportunity to try the M&M test for through-hikers: Drop an M&M on the ground. A day-hiker will pick it up and put it in his trash bag. A backpacker will wipe it off and eat it. A through-hiker will chase it down the mountainside.

How to Get There

From exit 53 off I-80, drive 0.6 mile to the traffic light in the town of Delaware Water Gap. Turn left (south) on

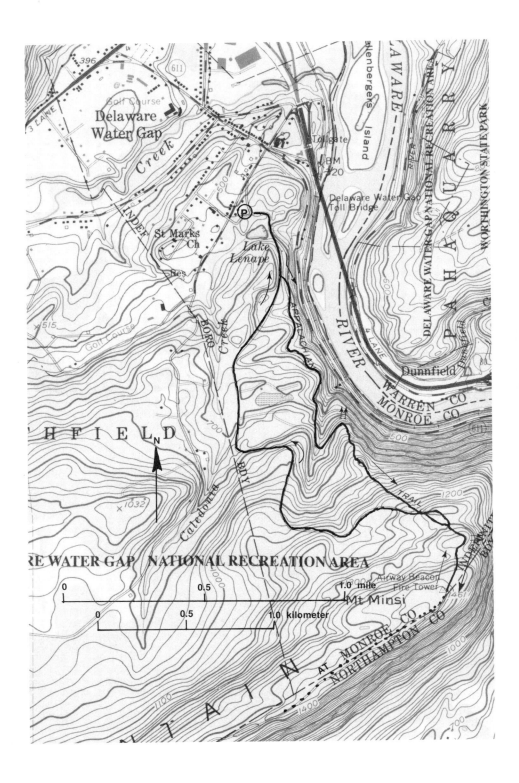

DELAWARE WATER GAP NATIONAL RECREATION AREA

Delaware Water Gap

PA 611 and go 0.3 mile. Then turn right at the Deer Head Inn onto Mountain Road; drive 0.2 mile to the Lake Lenape parking lot. Note the white blazes along Mountain Road, which show that it is part of the AT.

The Trail

From the parking lot, follow the white blazes past the gate on the Mount Minsi fire road. Just around the corner you cross the dam forming Lake Lenape, a picturesque small impoundment. Then the fire road passes cliffs to the right, and at 600 meters you follow the AT as it turns left on trail under hemlocks. Soon there is a view to your left of the Delaware, including the I-80 bridge. This bridge may be the scariest part of the AT; it shakes up and down whenever an 18-wheeler goes by.

Next, you encounter rhododendrons and hemlocks. Note that most of the hemlocks here look sick, presumably from the woolly adelgid, an aphid that sucks the juices from the hemlock needles, weakening the trees. Some trees die immediately; the larger specimens will provide picturesque snags for years to come. Others soldier on, but no one knows whether they will survive. The biodiversity of Penn's Woods is taking another hit.

Cross a larger stream on rocks at 1.8 km. This is the outlet for Lake Latini. At 2.0 km there is another view of the Water Gap, but note that the AT switchbacks to the right just before this view. Follow the blazes carefully, as the trail crosses open areas; sometimes the blazes are painted on the rock underfoot. There is another view of the Gap before the AT enters a tunnel through the rhododendrons.

Note the well-made water bars on this section. Some are made of rocks and others of logs. The purpose of a water bar is to deflect water off the trail. This means the upper edge must be cleared whenever it fills up with sand and mud. A well-made water bar is a thing of beauty and a chore forever.

The climb eases off before you jog left across the Mount Minsi fire road at 3.0 km. You reach your last view of the Gap at 3.3 km. Pitch pines and shadbush grow around these rocks, along with the only healthy hemlock I saw on this hike. From here you can see the cliffs and the other side of Mount Tammany; you can also see up Dunnfield Creek on the New Jersey side of the river. This is the last view, but not the summit. If you are a peak-bagger, continue along the AT for another 400 meters to the foundations of a fire tower. (The excursion to this, the actual summit, is included in this hike's mileage.)

While I was looking at the spruce trees growing at the summit, I noticed a movement at the edge of the brush. It was a bear—the only bear I've ever seen on the AT. When I made a motion for my camera, (s)he vanished into the woods.

Turn back along the AT, but when you reach the Mount Minsi fire road, bear right. Cross the AT again and continue down over ledges of bedrock. At various junctions along the way, just continue straight ahead. At 5.0 km pass a spring to the left. Black birch grows along the fire road. At 6.8 km there is a road to the left. It leads to a view of the Gap from a bluff, but is not included in this hike. The junction is marked only by some rusty culvert pipes. Next, the AT comes in from the right, and, finally, you pass Lake Lenape to reach the parking lot.

There is additional hiking at Big Pocono State Park, just a few exits up I-80 (see Hike 37).

33

Dingmans Falls

Location: 10 miles south of Milford

Distance: 8.0 km (4.9 miles)

Time: 4 hours

Vertical rise: 160 meters (525 feet)

Highlights: waterfalls

Map: USGS 7½' Lake Maskenozha

An obscure item in a tourist brochure sent me on a search for this hike. The brochure claimed there was a "five mile" hike at Dingmans Falls. But standard hiking references list only 0.5 mile there, and less than 2 at the George W. Childs Recreation Area farther upstream. I finally found the hike; it consists of the section of Dingmans Creek between the two areas.

The trail is unmarked, unmaintained, and unbuilt—yet it is easy to follow. All you have to do is keep the creek in sight. The woods are fairly open and in many places a footway has been worn into the ground, but this is a trail for the more adventurous hiker. Note that only the south bank of Dingmans Creek is public property. Private enclaves remain on the north bank, owned by hostile landowners.

The ideal time for this hike is a few days after a heavy rain. Beware of subfreezing weather, when spray from the falls can cover the steps and walkways with ice. There is some steep hillside walking on this hike, so wear your boots.

If it's open (April through October), take a look at the exhibits in the visitors center. These exhibits deal with the area's wildlife and geology. How did the Delaware Water Gap National Recreation Area get so many waterfalls? During the Ice Age, a river of ice deepened and widened the Delaware River Valley. It also confused the preglacial drainage system. When the ice melted, the new streams flowing off the Pocono Plateau flowed over cliffs to get to the Delaware Valley. Waterfalls are generally transient on a geologic time scale; these date from the most recent Ice Age, only 15,000 to 20,000 years ago. Waterfalls erode back upstream, creating a narrow canyon below.

How to Get There
This hike is written as an in-and-out hike, but it could also be done as a car shuttle. If you elect the latter option, first leave one car at the George W.

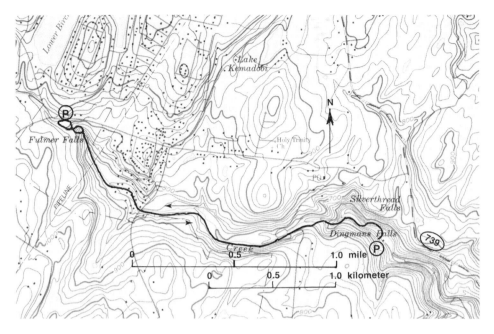

Childs Recreation Area. To get there, from the traffic light at the junction of US 209 and PA 739, drive north on PA 739 for 1.1 miles. Then turn left on Silver Lake Road, which is the first paved road on your left. After another 1.7 miles you reach the recreation site. There are two parking areas. Leave one car here and return to the junction of US 209 and PA 739. Turn south on US 209. At 0.1 mile from the light, turn right on Johnny Bee Road. After 0.4 mile, turn right on Dingmans Falls Road; it is another 0.8 mile to the visitors center and parking lot.

The Trail
Start your hike from the visitors center and cross the bridge over Dingmans Creek. Immediately you are at the foot of Silver Thread Falls, a narrow waterfall that has eroded along joint fractures in shale. Shale erodes relatively easily.

Then move on and cross the creek again. Turn right through a tunnel in the rhododendron (it blooms the first 2 weeks in July). Soon you reach the platform at the base of Dingmans Falls. The 40-meter fall cascades down shale ledges.

Now turn back and take the steps to the upper platform, crossing another bridge over a side stream. The upper platform is at the brink of Dingmans Falls. This is as far as most people go, but it is where the adventurous part of this hike begins.

Look for a path up the ledges, worn over the hemlock roots, and follow it. Soon your way becomes easier, but keep well above the creek. (You wouldn't want to slip and fall in, because swimming is prohibited this close to the falls.)

Since this trail is not blazed or maintained, there are frequently two or even three footways at different levels. Some of them are so wide that they look like somebody has actually done the required sidehill construction with Pulaskis and mattocks.

Soon the slope eases off and you can descend closer to the stream. At 1.2 km you cross Doodle Hollow Road. It is blocked to traffic at the bridge. Do *not* cross this bridge, as there is private land on the other side.

Later you reach an old grade that descends to the stream. Note that there is a ford here where people used to drive across.

The woods are open and the few blowdowns can be detoured or stepped over, but most of the trees are hemlocks. The woolly adelgid, an insect pest accidentally introduced, has already invaded the Delaware recreation area. It feeds on hemlocks and eventually kills them. If it were to kill the hemlocks here, brush would grow up and the valley would soon be blocked with blowdowns. The woolly adelgid has no known natural enemies.

At 2.6 km cross SR 2001, a paved road that to your right goes to Silver Lake Road and PA 739. Do *not* cross this bridge. Follow an old road briefly, but when it veers away from the creek, bear right and return to the bank. At 3.3 km, cross a pipeline swath. Another 100 meters brings you to the first bridge in the Childs park. This last bit is the steepest and hardest part of the hike.

Cross this bridge to get a good view of Deer Leap Falls. Then climb to its brink and cross again. Continue upstream and cross yet another bridge, below Fulmer Falls. Continue to Factory Falls. The crumbling stone walls are the postindustrial ruins of a factory that once got waterpower from Dingmans Creek. Cross a bridge above Factory Falls. There are no more falls above this point, so turn downstream, crossing bridges in the opposite direction.

There are one too many bridges for this plan to work out. Be sure that you end up on the *south* side of Dingmans Creek at the last bridge below Deer Leap Falls. (This is the right side as you face downstream.) Proceed downstream and retrace your steps to the visitors center and your car.

We are used to the roar of traffic, the roar of airplanes, the roar of machinery. A waterfall is a natural roar. As John Muir said, "As long as I live I'll hear waterfalls and birds sing and get as near the heart of the world as I can."

Tobyhanna Lake

34

Lakeside Trail

Location: near I-380 south of Scranton

Distance: 8.3 km (5.2 miles)

Time: 2½ hours

Vertical rise: 25 meters (80 feet)

Highlights: lake

Maps: USGS 7½' Tobyhanna; park map

Tobyhanna State Park on PA 423 outside the town of Tobyhanna is the site of this hike. The Lakeside Trail is a hardened path for hiking and bicycling in summer, snowmobiling and cross-country skiing in winter. It circles Tobyhanna Lake, formed by the damming of Tobyhanna Creek. This is a very easy trail to hike and you can look around to see things; you don't have to keep looking at the ground, as you do on most trails.

Tobyhanna State Park is part of the former Tobyhanna Military Reservation, which was used as an artillery range up through World War II. The area still contains unexploded shells; some are found every year. The trails

have been cleared, so this concern arises only for off-trail hikers. If you should find a shell, don't pick it up; mark its position as best you can and report it to the park office. Let the bomb disposal squad take care of the shell.

The Lakeside Trail is wheelchair-accessible, and some adventurous handicapped people have completed the entire trail. Walking shoes are fine for this hike's excellent footway, but you still may have to skirt a puddle or two.

How to Get There

Tobyhanna State Park is most easily reached from exit 7 off I-380. Take PA 423 north for about 3 miles to the park. You can also reach the park from exit 6 off I-84; follow PA 507, PA 191, and PA 423 for a total of 12 miles. At the entrance to the park, turn left for the day-use area. Park in area 2 or 3.

The Trail

Make your way to the bathhouse. Bear left past the water pump and continue on the surfaced trail, which follows the shore of Tobyhanna Lake around a point to the boat-launching and -mooring area. The trail is blue-blazed except right near the bathhouse. Keep right to stay on it. Watch for evidence

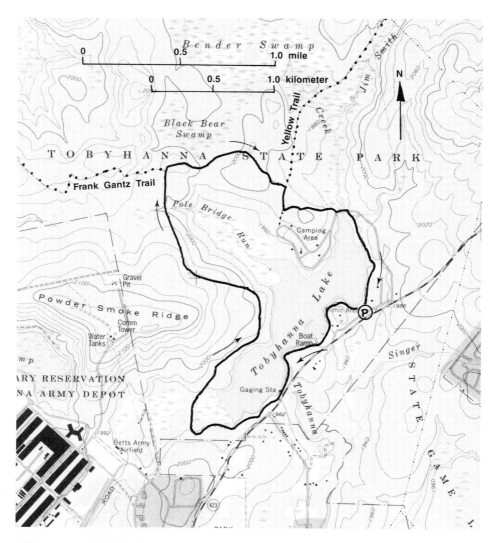

of beaver activity in the form of sticks with the bark chewed off or trees that have been felled. Here the Lakeside Trail is lined with rhododendrons.

At 1.4 km, you reach the dam; keep left and use the PA 423 bridge to cross the outlet. (Hikers are not permitted to use the walkway over the dam.) Then bear right and pass a vehicle gate to continue. Note the spruce growing along the trail. Beech is abundant and there are black cherry, yel-low birch, white birch, and red maple trees. Picnic tables are found along the way if you care to rest or eat lunch.

At 3.7 km you turn left, away from the lake. The trail is also equipped with mileposts set for snowmobiles, which circle the lake in the opposite direction. The muted roar of I-380, about 3 km away, can be heard.

Cross Pole Bridge Run on a sub-stantial bridge at 5.0 km, and reach the junction with the red-blazed Frank

Gantz Trail at 5.4 km. The Frank Gantz Trail connects with trails in Gouldsboro State Park, 5 km away. Blazed but not maintained, it could be used for a car-shuttle hike—or to combine this hike with the one at Gouldsboro (Hike 35) and create a 26 km boot-buster.

Turn right on the blue blazes. At 6.5 km, you reach a junction with the Yellow Trail. (This goes left 5.3 km all the way to PA 196, but it crosses Tobyhanna Creek without benefit of a bridge. The creek may be all but impassable in high water, but would make an inviting side trip in low water.)

Turn right on the blue blazes, then left to reach a parking lot at milepost 0, the start of the one-way snowmobile trail. Turn left on the paved road and cross a bridge consisting of five culverts over Tobyhanna Creek.

At 7.4 km, turn right on the Lakeside Trail and follow it back to the bathhouse and your car. In-season, take time for a swim.

Besides the Frank Gantz and Yellow Trails at Tobyhanna, there is additional hiking in nearby Gouldsboro State Park (see Hike 35).

Old 611

35

Gouldsboro State Park

Location: near I-380 south of Scranton

Distance: 9.1 km (5.6 miles)

Time: 3 hours

Vertical rise: 91 meters (300 feet)

Highlights: Pocono swamp

Maps: USGS 7½' Tobyhanna; park map

In 1949 Pennsylvania received title to 10,500 hectares from the federal government. This land had been part of the Tobyhanna Military Reservation. A third of the land was split between Tobyhanna and Gouldsboro State Parks, while the balance became State Game Lands 127.

Gouldsboro Park is named for the nearby town of Gouldsboro, which in turn was named for railroad magnate Jay Gould. At one time Gould owned 10 percent of all the railroads in the country, including the Erie-Lackawanna, which separates the two parks. This railroad is now part of Steamtown USA and is used for excursions from Scranton to Pocono Summit. Gould was also co-owner of a nearby tannery.

Although parts of this hike are on old roads, the Prospect Rock Trail is rough and rocky, requiring your boots. In addition, there is a challenging crossing of the outlet from Kistler Swamp.

How to Get There

Take exit 6 off I-380 and drive north on PA 507 for 2.1 miles. Turn south on the park road and go 1.0 mile; turn left into parking lot 1. Gouldsboro can also be reached from exit 6 off I-84 by driving about 8 miles south on PA 507.

The Trail

Pick up the blue-blazed Prospect Rock Trail and head north on an old road, easy walking. At 500 meters, turn left on trail to reach State Park Road. Cross the road, step over the guide rail, and turn right. Follow the road to 1.5 km, where you turn left on a very rocky trail that follows the northern boundary of the park. At several places you can look into backyards of houses built across the boundary on private land.

After the park boundary turns north, climb steeply over rocks to Prospect Rock (elevation: 628 meters). There

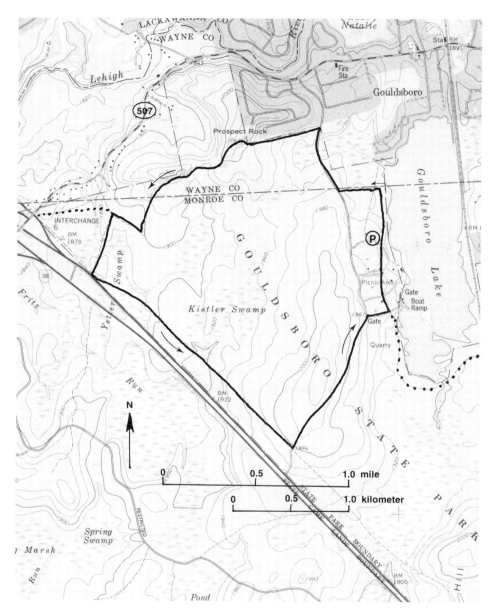

may have been a view to the south from here at one time, but the trees have grown up. Beyond, the trail descends gently, but the footway remains rocky.

At 3.6 km, turn sharply right on an old road. At last you have a good footway. Then turn left at the junction with the red-blazed Connector Trail. At 4.2 km you reach the outlet from Kistler Swamp. Cross here as best you can. On the far side of the stream, the footway becomes a watercourse in wet times, but at 4.5 km you reach Old

611 and turn left. The Connector Trail comes in from your right.

Old 611 is the remains of a paved two-lane highway that was replaced by I-380. The concrete is cracked, buckled, and broken now. As it heads south across Kistler Swamp, it has been reduced to a single lane by encroaching brush. Swamps such as this are a feature of the Poconos, a mighty fortress for black bears when they are hunted. No hunter would penetrate such a swamp very far, so the Poconos have the most secure bear population in the state. Beyond the swamp Old 611 gently climbs a hill with aspen trees.

As you hike down Old 611, ask yourself how much of our country is polluted with traffic noise. Pennsylvania is said to have more miles of highway than any other state except Texas—which is five times as large. Perhaps we could abandon some more. They make such nice trails after a couple of decades.

At 6.8 km, turn left on the old park entrance road, which was severed to the west by I-380. There is a picnic table at this junction. The old entrance road is in better shape than Old 611, although they must have been abandoned at the same time.

Continue to 8.2 km, where you pass a gate and turn right on a paved road to the boat launch. Next, turn left where the red-blazed Frank Gantz Trail comes in from Tobyhanna State Park. Walk through the picnic area, crossing several parking areas, to area 1, where you left your car.

Additional hiking is available at nearby Tobyhanna State Park (see Hike 34). The Frank Gantz Trail between the two parks is also available.

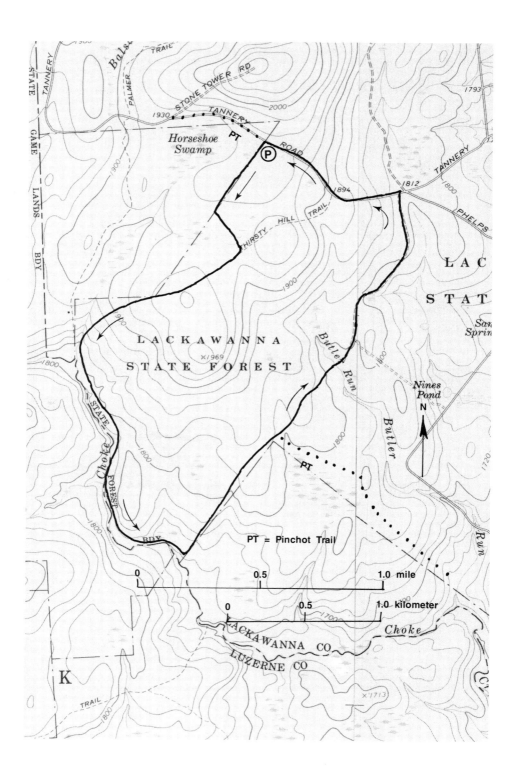

PT = Pinchot Trail

36

Choke Creek Trail

Location: 12 miles east of Wilkes-Barre

Distance: 10.0 km (6.2 miles)

Time: 3¼ hours

Vertical rise: 90 meters (290 feet)

Highlights: mountain stream

Maps: USGS 7½' Pleasant View Summit, Thornhurst; Pinchot Trail map

Choke Creek Nature Trail is on the southern part of the Pinchot Trail in Lackawanna State Forest. The Pinchot Trail System was laid out by Frank Gantz, a retired truck driver, back in the 1970s. He explored the area, finding old trails and new routes, determining where the trail should go.

As usual, there are lots of wet spots and more than a few rocks on the trail, so your hiking boots are in order.

How to Get There

For directions to the Pinchot Trail, see Hike 44, Painter Creek Loop.

If you are coming from I-380 or I-80, turn left on Tannery Road just 0.1 mile north of the junction of Pine Grove and Bear Lake Roads. From I-81, continue 2.4 miles past the Pinchot trailhead and turn right onto Tannery Road. In either case, drive 1.9 miles to a parking area on the left with a large sign proclaiming CHOKE CREEK NATURE TRAIL. On Tannery Road you will cross the blue blazes of the main Pinchot Trail. The length of Choke Creek Trail is greater than is advertised on the sign.

The Trail

Start down the blue-blazed trail that leads directly away from the road; it follows the boundary of state forest land. Along the way you pass mountain and sheep laurel (both bloom in June), rhododendron (blooms in July), black spruce, and white pine.

Turn left at 600 meters and detour around a bog. Here there are many highbush blueberries. They ripen in July, but many of the berry pickers wear fur coats, even in summer.

Turn right at 1.2 km and pass pitch pine, black gum, red maple, black birch, and sassafras. The leaves of sassafras are quite variable. Some leaves are elliptical, while others are mitten shaped—both left-handed and right-handed. Some leaves even have "thumbs" on both sides.

Cross a stream on stepping-stones at 1.8 km, and turn left at a campsite. In May look for painted trillium along the trail. Also listen for the towhee, or woods robin. Towhees scratch noisily among the dead leaves on the forest floor. Their most frequent call is a loud *chewink,* but at times they will sing *drink your tea,* with the "tea" trilled.

Now beech trees, another northern hardwood, make their appearance along the trail. Beech leaves are sometimes confused with American chestnut leaves but tend to be shorter.

At 3.5 km, turn downstream along a tributary of Choke Creek. Immediately you reach the main stream at a beaver pond; you can see the beaver house. It appears that the dam was torn open by floods (probably on January 19, 1996), then repaired with a lot of broken branches, in addition to beaver-chewed logs. Part of a footbridge has also been incorporated into the repairs. At one point the pond has flooded the trail, and you must detour around it. A blazed tree is now surrounded by water, too. Choke Creek is alleged to harbor native brook trout.

Turn right at 3.9 km, passing one campsite, then another, farther along. Neither satisfies the requirement that campsites be at least 50 meters from any trail. Pass a large hemlock at 5.0 km and then what looks like an old burn area.

After passing another campsite at the edge of a pool, turn left and climb away from the creek along a posted boundary of private land. Cross a stream on stepping-stones and reach a junction with the Butler Run Trail at 6.8 km. The blue-blazed main trail of the Pinchot system turns right here, but you continue ahead on a red-blazed trail. Cross Butler Run at 7.5 km, and turn left on a grassy road at 7.8 km.

Suddenly a small, furry black animal darts across the trail ahead. It's a bear cub trying to catch up with its family. Leave bear cubs alone. The mother is not far off. No matter how cute it is, don't touch the cub. If it smells "wrong," its mother may abandon it. Bear adoptions are difficult to arrange, and a cub raised in captivity is sentenced to a life behind bars.

Along the grassy swath, you pass parts of the Howley Orienteering Area. This area was developed by a local search-and-rescue expert to teach skills required to avoid getting lost in the woods. At 9.0 km, pass a steel gate and turn left on Tannery Road. It is another 1 km back to your car.

The Pinchot Trail System provides lots of other hiking opportunities, particularly circuit hikes. See the Painter Creek Loop (Hike 44), for example.

37

Big Pocono State Park

Location: near I-80 west of Stroudsburg

Distance: 11.1 km (6.9 miles)

Time: 4 hours

Vertical rise: 295 meters (970 feet)

Highlights: views

Maps: USGS 7½' Mount Pocono; park map

Big Pocono State Park is on Camelback Mountain at the eastern edge of the Poconos. The mountain's steep north face is used as the Camelback Ski Area. The area was purchased by the Pennsylvania Game Commission. In 1953, however, 529 hectares became Big Pocono State Park. The remainder, just west of the park, is State Game Lands 38.

Parts of this hike are very steep and rocky, so wear your hiking boots.

How to Get There
The trailhead for this circuit hike is on Railroad Drive, just south of the park. Take exit 45 off I-80, west of Stroudsburg. Turn south on PA 715 and drive 0.4 mile; turn onto the second road to the right. This is Railroad Drive; there is a sign at this junction. Follow the drive for 1.2 miles, past the Growing Concern School, and park on the right at the junction with an abandoned railroad grade.

The Trail
Start your hike by heading down the railroad grade. Note poison ivy growing along the side. At 500 meters, dodge around a steel gate that limits vehicular access to the grade—although you can see where ATVs have bypassed the gate. This was once the grade of the Wilkes-Barre and Eastern Railroad, which carried coal from the anthracite fields to eastern markets. Some of this coal can still be seen on the grade.

The grade continues across fills, through cuts, and along the base of cliffs. It is marked with occasional blue blazes that face *in* instead of *along* the trail, but you will have no problem following the old grade. You can really move along through open woods of maple, hemlock, black birch, oak, and white pine, even though you are climbing.

Turn left on the orange-blazed

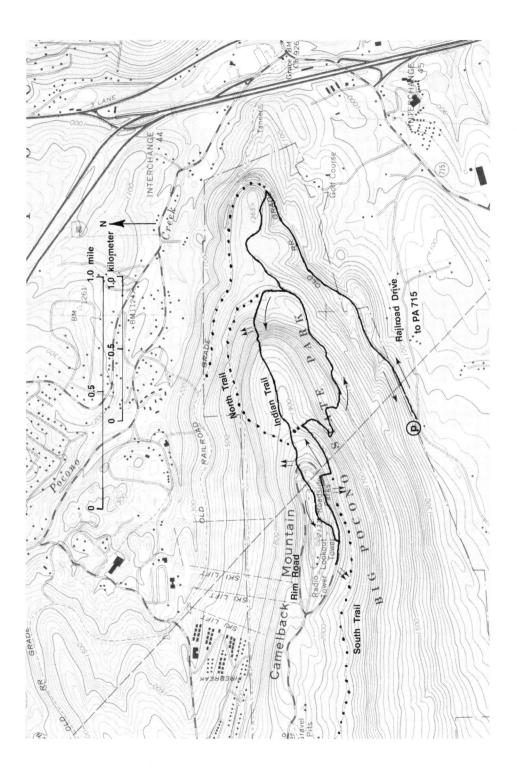

Trail on Camelback

Indian Trail at 2.0 km. (The railroad grade enters a deep cut in solid rock just ahead, so you can't miss this junction even though there is no sign.) Ignore an ATV trail to the right and climb on this old wagon road. Note the reddish shale outcrops in the road. At 2.6 km there is a pond to the left.

Shadbush grows along the trail at all levels up to the summit.

You reach a junction with the South Trail (on which you will return) at 2.9 km. For now, bear right on the Indian Trail. At last there are some signs to confirm that you are indeed on the right trail.

At 3.1 km, just after an open area, you reach an obscure but critical trail junction: The North Trail continues on the old road but the Indian Trail turns left onto a footpath. There are more orange blazes now and a sign at this junction. The ascent along the North Trail would avoid the steep climbs on the Indian Trail, but you would also miss the clifftop views along the Indian. The trail is difficult to follow and will challenge your path-finding skill.

The steep climb is over at 3.4 km and there is a series of views to the right from the top of the cliff you just climbed. At one end you can see the Delaware Water Gap; as you move along you can see far up into the Poconos toward Tobyhanna State Park and the Delaware State Forest.

Continue on the Indian Trail, which is now much easier to follow as it passes around and over boulders. Mountain laurel, pitch pine, and scrub oak grow here. Turn right at a large boulder at 3.8 km onto a grassy path studded with rocks. This is the first hump of the camel's back.

Next, the South Trail comes in from the left at a convenient bench. Then the North Trail comes in from the right. Stay on the Indian Trail. At 4.5 km, you reach Rim Road and another view to the right.

At the farthest advance of the last ice sheet, some 15,000 to 20,000 years ago, Camelback formed a promontory into the ice. The ice sheet stretched off to the west as well as south to the Delaware Water Gap; it must have been an impressive sight. Camelback is capped with a resistant conglomerate of Devonian age (350 million years old). Conglomerate looks like concrete in that it is made up of smaller rocks cemented together.

Continue across Rim Road and a parking lot to a trail that leads past a drinking fountain, then past small white birch trees. The trail enters a picnic area and leads to the old concession stand and the former park office. This is the second hump of the camel's back. (Evidently it was a Bactrian camel.)

Turn left at a sign for the South Trail and follow it to parking lot 3 and another picnic area. Turn right along Rim Road and walk 300 meters to dramatic views of the Allegheny Front in the southwest. Then return, passing views of the level crest of Blue Mountain. From west to east you can see Lehigh Gap, Little Gap, Wind Gap, and the Water Gap—probably the most famous geographic feature in eastern Pennsylvania. I can't understand why these views aren't better known. Even on a 4th of July weekend there was hardly anybody here. Big Pocono has been listed by the Bureau of Parks as one of the 30 best-kept secrets in Pennsylvania's park system.

Follow Rim Road past red pines to the Vista Trail. There isn't much vista anymore, but follow this trail down to the South Trail.

Turn left and follow the birch-lined South Trail to a junction at 6.6 km. Turn right and descend gently on switchbacks. Black birch and chestnut oak grow along the South Trail. Pass a spring and a vernal pond, both on your left.

Bear right on the Indian Trail at 8.2 km and follow it back to the old railroad grade. Turn right and retrace your steps to Railroad Drive.

Another hike in the vicinity of Big Pocono State Park is Mount Minsi in the Delaware Water Gap (Hike 32). A hike in State Game Lands 38, just west of Big Pocono, is described in *Pennsylvania Hiking Trails*, 11th edition.

38

Boulder Field

Location: Hickory Run State Park, near the junction of I-80 and PA 9

Distance: 11.3 km (7.0 miles)

Time: 4 hours

Vertical rise: 170 meters (560 feet)

Highlights: boulder field

Maps: USGS 7½' Hickory Run; park map

The existence of Hickory Run State Park is due to Colonel H.C. Trexler, who purchased over 5000 hectares at tax sales after logging for timber and hemlock bark was completed in 1912. The National Park Service was able to acquire much of the park from his estate. During the 1930s this park and four others were operated as demonstration recreation areas by the National Park Service. In 1945 Hickory Run was deeded to the State of Pennsylvania. Other large parks in the state—Blue Knob, French Creek, Laurel Hill, Raccoon Creek—were acquired in the same manner. At 6250 hectares, Hickory Run is the largest state park in the Poconos and, indeed,

in eastern Pennsylvania.

It encompasses the boulder field that is your destination for this hike. The field was produced 15,000 to 20,000 years ago, when the glacial front of the last Ice Age was about 1.5 km to the northeast. (The terminal moraine of the Wisconsin ice sheet passes through Hickory Run.) The climate must have been like that of parts of Greenland near its ice cap today. Freezing and thawing would have been severe during the summer; water seeping into cracks would have frozen every night, wedging the rocks apart. Subsequent water erosion has removed any sand and gravel, leaving only the boulders.

How to Get There

To reach the trailhead, take exit 41 off I-80 and turn east onto PA 534. Turn left in Lehigh Tannery and continue across a section of State Game Lands 40. Then enter Hickory Run State Park, passing the park office. Immediately after passing under the Pennsylvania Turnpike, park on the left side of the highway at 9.8 miles.

Hickory Run State Park can also be reached from exit 35 off the Pennsylvania Turnpike by driving west 3 miles on PA 940 and then east on PA 534.

The distance, time, and vertical rise

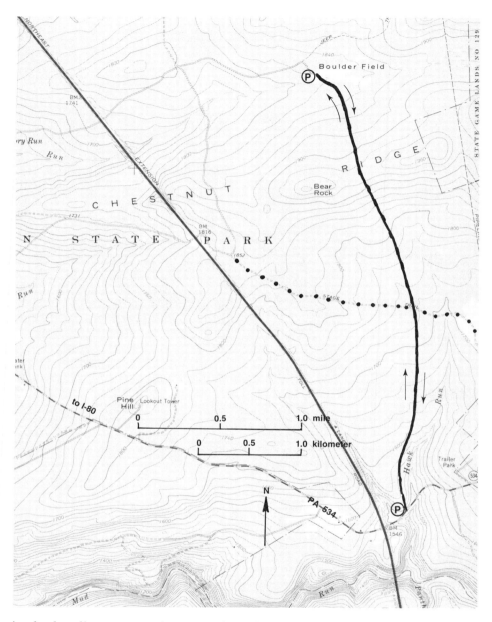

in the heading assume that you take this hike on an in-and-out basis, but if you have two cars available, you can also do it as a car-shuttle hike by leaving a car at the Boulder Field parking area. To reach this area, follow a park road that leaves PA 534 from a spot

0.5 mile east of the park office. The drive is 7.9 miles.

The Trail
The Boulder Field Trail leaves from the corner of the parking area on PA 534. The trail heads up a flight of

Boulder field

steps and then crosses an old apple orchard before entering the woods. It's unblazed but wide and easy to follow as it slowly diverges from the roar of the turnpike. Trees along the way are beech, black cherry, red maple, hemlock, yellow birch, black gum, and a very occasional red oak—typical mixed hardwoods. There are scattered clumps of rhododendrons along the first part of the trail. It is a very pleasant walk through the woods, although the footway is rocky. Farther along there are scattered hemlocks.

You cross the Stage Trail at 2.5 km. Once a stage route from Philadelphia to Wilkes-Barre, today it is a wide trail that traverses the park. However, it is open to vehicles.

Beyond the Stage Trail, the Boulder Field Trail becomes narrower, crosses a watercourse, and passes through patches of mountain laurel. Hemlocks become more numerous. Spruce, black gum, and white pine

trees are also passed. Under the white pines, stop and listen to the wind in the treetops.

The official trail description says there is a steady uphill slope, but it is scarcely noticeable. At 4.4 km, you cross the flat top of Chestnut Ridge and start to descend very gently through a dense stand of hemlocks into the headwaters of Hickory Run itself. You can also see old yellow and red paint blazes along the trail.

The edge of the boulder field is reached at 5.3 km. The field occupies a relatively flat valley at the headwaters of Hickory Run. Sometimes water can be heard running underneath the rocks.

As you head out into the field, take a good look at where you emerged from the woods. On my last hike this spot was marked only by a signboard leaning against a tree. You will need to find this trailhead to return to your car. The listed distance takes you clear across the field to the parking lot, where your other car will be if you did this hike as a shuttle. Otherwise, retrace your steps down the Boulder Field Trail to your car on PA 534.

Other hiking opportunities abound at Hickory Run State Park, as there are 60 km of trails. In particular, see Hawk Falls (Hike 28), Skyline Trail (Hike 29), and Fourth Run Trail (Hike 45).

39

Pennel Run

Location: west of PA 402, north of Stroudsburg

Distance: 11.4 km (7.1 miles)

Time: 4¼ hours

Vertical rise: 220 meters (730 feet)

Highlights: natural area

Maps: USGS 7½' Twelvemile Pond, Skytop; Thunder Swamp Trail System map

The Thunder Swamp Trail System (TSTS) in the Delaware State Forest provides over 70 km of hiking trails. The system includes a blue-blazed loop trail and numerous red-blazed side trails, and provides recreational opportunities in rapidly growing Pike County.

The Pennel Run Natural Area consists of 380 hectares of aspens, black birches, and mixed oaks. Much of Utts Swamp lies within the natural area.

This hike also visits Spruce Run, which flows east of the natural area. Like most other streams in the Poconos, its tea-colored waters flow through a corridor of hemlocks.

This portion of the Thunder Swamp Trail is unusually rocky, so wear your hiking boots.

How to Get There

You can reach the trailhead from exit 8 off I-84 by driving south on PA 402 for 14.7 miles, passing Porters Lake and the Burnt Mills trailhead of the TSTS. Turn right onto Snow Hill Road and follow it for 2.4 miles to a parking lot on the right.

You can also reach Snow Hill Road from exit 52 off I-80. Follow US 209 north to Marshalls Creek and turn onto PA 402. Follow PA 402 north, passing the main TSTS trailhead, and turn left on Snow Hill Road after about 10.5 miles.

The Trail

Turn right on paved Snow Hill Road and go 50 meters, then turn right again onto the blue-blazed main trail. Pass a trail register and an American chestnut sprout. After the logging of the 19th century, the Appalachians returned to hardwoods. From Maine to Georgia, every other tree was an American chestnut. Then came the chestnut blight, an imported fungus. The blight does not kill the below-ground portions of the tree, so stumps continue

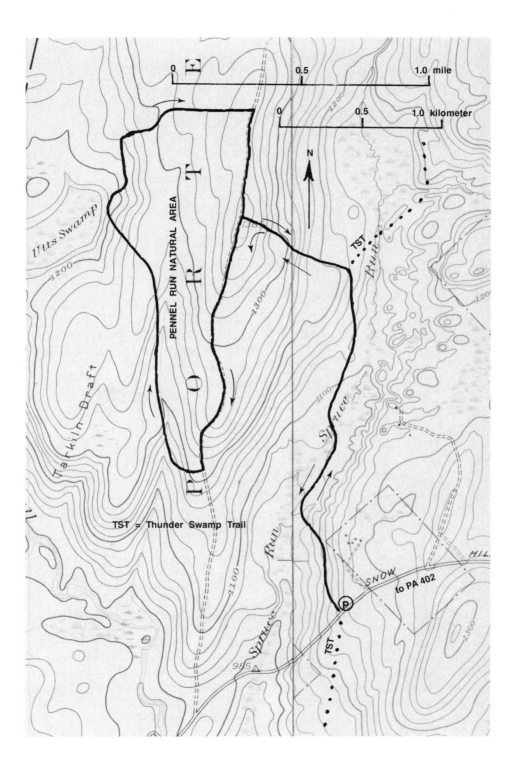

TST = Thunder Swamp Trail

Bridge over Spruce Run

to send up new shoots even today. Indeed, the abundance of these shoots keeps the chestnut from being designated an endangered species! However, many experts suspect that the old chestnut stumps are now about to die. Then the American chestnut—an ideal forest tree with wood for both rough and fine construction and nuts for both people and wildlife—will be extinct at last. Perhaps then it can be classed as endangered.

At 800 meters, pass some large white pines. Beech, shagbark hickory, tulip, and hemlock also grow here. Spruce Run can be seen to the left. There is some poison ivy along the trail near Spruce Run.

Cross a side stream and come to a bridge over Spruce Run. This bridge was built by volunteers in the Trail Care Project of the Keystone Trails Association (KTA). The first year they carried in wire baskets, called gabions, and filled them with locally grown rocks. The gabions stood here for 11 months before Trail Care was able to return and finish the bridge.

Continue on the blue blazes and climb gently to an intersection at 2.6 km, marked by a trail sign. All the trail signs along this hike were made by KTA volunteers; many were installed by an expedition in April 1991.

Turn left on red blazes at this junction and climb gently, except for a ledge, to Hay Road. This trail is so straight that it must have been a fire lane in the early days of the state forests. Hay Road is red-blazed in both directions and forms the eastern boundary of the Pennel Run Natural Area. Turn left and follow this delightful old road along the crest of the ridge. In May look for wild azaleas and pink lady's slippers.

Turn right on a trail at 4.8 km and follow it down to Pennel Run, which you cross on moss-covered rocks. On the far side, turn upstream and follow blazes carefully. The trail crosses another ridge and descends to the edge of Utts Swamp. It then climbs back up the ridge to Hay Road at 7.7 km. Turn right and close the loop at 8.0 km. Turn left on the old fire lane and retrace your steps to your car, remembering to turn right on the blue blazes.

Other hiking opportunities nearby include the Thunder Swamp Trail (Hike 43) and Big Bear Swamp (Hike 41). For a free trail map of the Thunder Swamp Trail System, write to Delaware State Forest, PO Box 150, Stroudsburg, PA 18360; or call 717-424-3001.

40

Bruce Lake Natural Area

Location: between Promised Land
State Park and I-84

Distance: 11.8 km (7.4 miles)

Time: 3½ hours

Vertical rise: 98 meters (320 feet)

Highlights: glacial lake

Maps: USGS 7 ½' Promised Land;
park map

The Bruce Lake Natural Area in the
Delaware State Forest is just north of
Promised Land State Park. It contains
a glacial lake and several swamps. It is
a sample of northern New England
and Canada set in the Mid-Atlantic
states.

Bruce Lake itself has no cottages,
no roads, no outboard motors, and—
unless you carry one in—no boats.
Yes, Ontario has 250,000 lakes, but
this one is ours. The trails are blue-
blazed and have good footing.

If you stuck to the old roads now
reverting to trails, you could get by
with walking shoes, but this hike includes a circuit of Bruce Lake itself,
where your boots will help you with
the rocks.

How to Get There
There are two access points to the
Bruce Lake Natural Area along PA
390. This hike uses the northern one,
which is just 0.1 mile south of exit 7
off I-84. The Egypt Meadows parking
area is on your left.

The Trail
Pass the gate on blue-blazed Egypt
Meadows Road and head into the
woods, passing a trail register and a
carsonite trail sign. Land managers
are enamored of carsonite posts, but
I find them lacking in aesthetic value
compared to the old-fashioned wooden
sign. We'll see what they look like in
10 years; already some of the decals
are flaking off. After even 20 years, a
well-made routed wooden sign may
look a bit scruffy, but it will still be
perfectly legible.

Next, pass the Snow Shoe Trail on
your right and then a small swamp to
your left. At 400 meters, turn right on
Panther Swamp Road. Then bear right
at a junction with the blue-blazed Egypt
Meadows Trail, which provides a way
to vary your return (see the map). Egypt

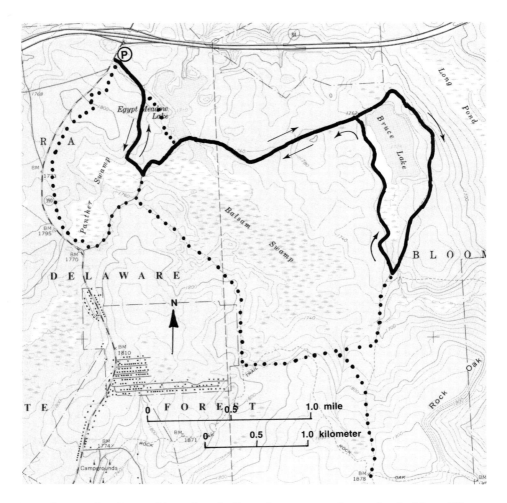

Meadows Lake, formed by a dam built by the Civilian Conservation Corps, can be seen through the trees.

Panther Swamp Road passes over a low hill. Note the sheep laurel growing along this section. Panther Swamp is visible to your right.

Turn left on Bruce Lake Road at 1.4 km. The small bridge visible to your right crosses the outlet from Panther Swamp. Next, you pass the other end of Egypt Meadows Trail, then reach a bridge across the narrows of Egypt Meadows Lake. On my last visit, I found water flowing across the approach to the bridge. There had just been a lot of rain and I thought little of it until I noticed that the lake levels were different above and below the bridge. Peering under the bridge on the high side, I couldn't see a thing—the water level was up to the bottom of the bridge. But from the low side I found that beavers had built their dam under the bridge, raising the level of the southern part of Egypt Meadows Lake by half a meter! These animals have produced a pond of unusual size.

Continue east on Bruce Lake Road,

passing witch hazel bushes. This shrub blooms in the fall, starting in September and continuing after all its leaves have fallen and the snow is flying.

Beyond, you can see a low cliff through the trees with a large white pine growing in the scant layer of soil on top. This cliff was produced by a glacier "plucking" blocks of rock from the "downstream" side of the ledge. The rock froze to the moving ice and broke off along bedding planes and joints as the glacier moved.

At 3.9 km, you reach the junction with the West Branch of the Bruce Lake Trail on your right. Camping is no longer permitted at Bruce Lake. Continue ahead and you'll see Bruce Lake between the trees. There are a number of side trails leading to the lakeshore.

Look for a patch of bedrock near the north end of the lake. It is marked with scratches called glacial striations, which show the direction of motion of the ice and were caused by rocks frozen in the bottom of the ice sheet. Here at Bruce Lake the ice may have been a kilometer in depth, but it moved only centimeters per day.

The bedrock is exposed here now because the soil was burned off by forest fires after the region was logged. If the bedrock had not been protected by the soil, the striations would have weathered away thousands of years ago.

Continue east on the old road, passing a junction with an unmarked trail. The Bruce Lake Trail swings around to the south and passes a disabled water pump. Beyond, the East Branch of the Bruce Lake Trail narrows to a real trail. At one time this trail was blazed yellow; it has been reblazed blue, but a few of the old yellow blazes survive. The footway is excellent. It is far enough back from the lake to stay dry and relatively free of rocks.

On a recent visit I had to stop suddenly in my tracks to watch a buck with a magnificent rack bound across the trail in front of me. I had been moving upwind, so he didn't smell or hear my approach.

The southern part of the lake becomes a swamp and the trail continues south on higher ground before edging to the west. At 6.3 km you reach a short but welcome bridge over the outlet from Bruce Lake. Just beyond is the junction with the West Branch Trail.

You could extend your hike here by turning left and following the Bruce Lake, Rock Oak, and Brown Trails encircling Balsam Swamp.

However, on this hike you turn right on the West Branch and follow it back to Bruce Lake Road. The West Branch is rockier than the East and has a couple of wet spots. Turn left on Bruce Lake Road and retrace your steps to the bridge over the Egypt Meadows Lake narrows. Just beyond, you could vary your return by turning right on the Egypt Meadows Trail. Otherwise, retrace your steps via the Panther Swamp Trail to your car on PA 390.

Other hiking opportunities can be found at Promised Land State Park (Hike 42) and on the Blooming Grove Trail System north of exit 8 off PA 402 (Hike 30).

41

Big Bear Swamp

Location: east of PA 402, north of Stroudsburg

Distance: 14.2 km (8.8 miles)

Time: 5¼ hours

Vertical rise: 220 meters (730 feet)

Highlights: natural area

Maps: USGS 7½' Twelvemile Pond, Lake Maskenozha; Thunder Swamp Trail System map

The Thunder Swamp Trail System in the Delaware State Forest was built by the Youth Conservation Corps (YCC) in the 1970s. It covers a variety of terrain in the Poconos, from dry ridges to swamps, wetlands, and streams. Actually, there is no Thunder Swamp, but the YCC members liked the name.

Routine maintenance is performed by state forest workers and volunteers from the Pocono Outdoor Club. Rectangular blazes are used to mark the trails—blue for the main trail, red for side trails. Most intersections are marked with trail signs, many of which were made by Keystone Trails Asso-

ciation volunteers and installed during an April 1991 expedition.

Public lands in the Poconos are contorted into gerrymanders. At various places the trails must thread narrow corridors of public land or take circuitous detours to avoid private land.

The many swamps in the Poconos result from the glaciation of the area 15,000 to 20,000 years ago. Preglacial valleys were blocked with glacial debris, so many areas were poorly drained. The swamps today are filled with rhododendron and black spruce, making them all but impenetrable to humans but providing a refuge for bears. The bear population in the Poconos is the most secure of all regions in the state. Human residents of the Poconos seem to get on fairly well with the bears, even when one is hibernating under their deck. You aren't guaranteed of seeing bears on this hike—but they will know you are here.

People aren't the only creatures who use trails; so do bears, deer, and coyotes. Look for their scat along the trails. Coyote and fox scat will frequently be deposited on top of a rock to say, "This is *my* trail."

Big Bear Swamp, the site of this hike, is located in the Stillwater Natural Area. The 780 hectares were logged

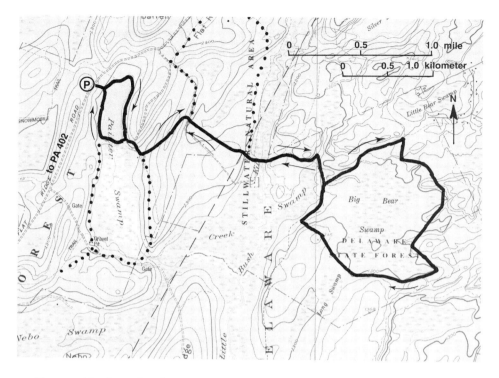

and burned before they became state forest.

Rocks grow wild in the Poconos with their hard, sharp ends up, and wet spots are plentiful; wear your hiking boots.

How to Get There

The trailhead is a parking lot on Flat Ridge Road. It can be reached from exit 8 off I-84 by driving south on PA 402 for 10.6 miles. Then turn left on paved Old Bushkill Road (SR 2003) and drive 1.6 miles. Turn left on gravel Flat Ridge Road and continue for 2.2 miles to the parking area on the right.

The trailhead can also be reached from exit 52 off I-80. Follow US 209 north to Marshalls Creek and turn north onto PA 402. Continue on PA 402 to Old Bushkill Road, at the Burnt Mills trailhead. Finally, you can reach it from the blinker on US 209 in Bushkill by turning north onto Old Bushkill Road.

The Trail

Start your hike by heading down the red-blazed trail at the edge of the parking lot. Soon you pass a trail register. (I found three trail registers on this hike, but not one was in serviceable shape.)

At 170 meters, keep left for the Stillwater Natural Area. The trail circles Painter Swamp. The name probably refers to *Felis concolor,* the mountain lion, or panther. Spruces and large white pines, together with highbush blueberries—a favorite summer food of bears—grow along the trail. Also look for sheep laurel.

At 1.1 km you reach the corner of a dam that has raised the water level in Painter Swamp to form a pond. Jog left 20 meters on a jeep road and continue on the red-blazed trail to a junction at 1.4 km. Turn left on the blue-blazed main trail here. Shortly, the trail jogs right for 45 meters before continuing. Watch the blazes carefully here.

Cross Coon Swamp Road at 2.2 km. There is a junction with a red-blazed trail that makes a loop through the northern part of the Stillwater Natural Area, returning to the blue-marked trail at 2.9 km. This loop is not included in this hike, but it is an option; it would add about 4 km to your total distance. For this hike, though, follow the blue blazes and, at 3.1 km, cross a bridge over Little Bush Kill Creek. Next, the trail picks up an old woods road through mountain laurel. Follow it to 3.8 km, where you turn left on trail. (Ahead, the old road would cross a corner of private land.)

Cross a stream on rocks and continue to an unsigned trail junction at 4.2 km. Here the blue blazes go in both directions in order to circle Big Bear Swamp. Turn left on the woods road and follow it past the first of many rock ledges around the swamp. At 4.8 km, turn right on trail, passing white pines and black spruces.

Turn left at 6.5 km past hemlocks and more spruces. Look for painted trilliums here in May. Then cross a log bridge. There are some stone steps at 7.4 km. Look for bear scat around the borders of the swamp.

If you wish to enter the swamp, be prepared to get your feet wet, and be absolutely sure to take your compass. It is very easy to go around in circles.

At 9.1 km, turn right on the old woods road you followed earlier. Soon you reach a heavily posted border of private land. Cross the outlet from Big Bear Swamp at 9.8 km. You can either rock-hop on the old road or detour downstream to a bridge.

At 10.0 km, you close the loop around Big Bear Swamp. Note the three blazes on a rock in the trail. Turn left and retrace your steps to the bridge over Little Bush Kill. About 1.5 km of the creek meander through state forest land. These are the "stillwaters" of the natural area's name.

Continue to retrace your steps to the junction of blue- and red-marked trails at 12.8 km. Turn right on the red and follow the blazes carefully, avoiding a trail that climbs the hill.

At the edge of Painter Swamp, turn left and walk across the dam. See where it washed out and was rebuilt by beavers. Part of this section is bridged, but the rest can be very wet in high water. The far side of the dam affords the best views of Painter Swamp.

At 13.3 km, turn right at a signed junction of red-blazed trails. Pass a campsite and continue to 14.1 km, another junction of red-blazed trails. Turn left to return to the parking lot on Flat Ridge Road.

The Thunder Swamp Trail System offers many additional hiking opportunities; see Hikes 39 and 43.

42

Promised Land State Park

Location: south of exit 7 off I-84

Distance: 14.2 km (8.8 miles)

Time: 4¾ hours

Vertical rise: 110 meters (360 feet)

Highlights: lake, evergreens

Maps: USGS 7½' Promised Land; park map

Promised Land State Park, in the heart of the Poconos, was opened to the public in 1905. However, many of the park's facilities were not built until Civilian Conservation Corps (CCC) manpower became available in the Great Depression. From May 1933 until July 1941, Promised Land State Park was also known as Camp Pocono and Camp S-139. A company of the CCC was established in the present Deerfield and Pickerel Point Campgrounds.

Many worthwhile conservation and recreational projects were carried out during these years. The CCC men built fire roads and trails, reforested the terrain, established campgrounds

(over 500 sites are now available in four campgrounds), and constructed picnic pavilions and bathhouses. In addition, they built 12 rustic cabins still in use on Bear Wallow Road.

If you look around the park, you can find more evidence of the CCC era. The park museum, too, contains photographs and artifacts.

The Promised Land name was bestowed sarcastically by Shakers who had been promised riches from the wilderness. When they arrived in 1878, they found the ground filled with rocks and boulders. They soon departed, leaving only the name.

You will want your hiking boots for this long trail, with its many rocks and wet areas. All the trails in the park are blazed blue. If you see paint blazes of other colors, ignore them.

How to Get There

Promised Land can be reached from exit 7 off I-84. Drive south on PA 390 for 2.9 miles. Then turn left on North Shore Road and go 0.3 mile to a small parking area on the left side of the road.

The Trail

Head into the woods on the Rock Oak Ridge Trail, a woods road. Cross an intermittent stream and reach a junction with the Boundary Trail. This junction, like others in the park, is marked with carsonite posts bearing the names of the trails, icons identifying permissible users (hikers, snowmobilers, horses, and so on), and mysterious numbers. (The numbers are to be identified on a map available in 1997.) Note the sheep laurel growing near this junction. Its pink flowers blooming in the spring are much smaller than those of the more familiar mountain laurel, which you soon pass through as well.

Continue at 1.0 km on the Telephone Trail, which follows the path of a former telephone line, leaving the woods road behind. (The Telephone Trail is very rocky. You can avoid it by continuing on the Rock Oak Ridge Trail, then turning right on the Bruce

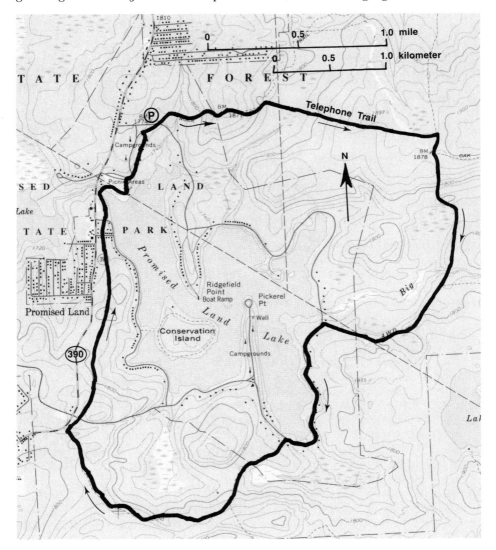

Promised Land Lake

Lake Trail—but at the cost of lengthening your hike.) Next, pass a peat bog to the left of the trail and reach a junction with the Whittaker Trail. At 2.5 km, jump from rock to rock as the trail crosses a woodland pool amid highbush blueberry.

Turn right on the Bruce Lake Trail at 2.9 km. This trail has a much better footway, courtesy of the CCC. Soon you reach a section of evergreens: hemlocks first, then white pines, spruces, and rhododendrons. Next, cross a footbridge over Big Inlet and turn right on the Big Inlet Trail— actually a gated woods road. This trail is also known as the Lake Laura Road.

At 5.7 km you reach another junction with the Boundary Trail. This trail could be used to avoid the road walking that lies ahead, but it is poorly marked and unmaintained. So proceed to paved North Shore Road at 5.9 km and turn left. Here there are larch and spruce trees, and views of Promised Land Lake.

Just before crossing Burley Inlet, you will spot the Short Trail to your left; ignore it. Turn left at 7.5 km on the Burley Inlet Trail. Keep left at a junction of woods roads to reach yet another Boundary Trail junction. Continue ahead on the Burley Inlet Trail, passing a junction with the Snow Shanty Trail at 9.4 km. Then pass through a clearing and continue to a gate. Turn right just beyond to reach a junction with the Rhododendron Trail, a snowmobile trail in-season. It is marked with orange diamonds nailed to the trees.

At 10.5 km, cross Pickerel Point Road. The park office and a public telephone are on the far side of PA 390. The Rhododendron Trail, often lined with dense stands of this shrub, continues north between Promised Land Lake to your right and PA 390 to your left. It passes a white pine plantation just before crossing Park

Avenue at 12.8 km. The trail passes between several cottages at this point.

Walk behind the boat rental (outhouses to your right) and cross the dam forming Promised Land Lake at 13.2 km. The route, without benefit of blazes, becomes more difficult to follow beyond, but head between the picnic area and swimming beach to a paved parking lot. At the far end, follow a gated but paved old road that leads to the Pines Campground. Continue to the far end of the campground and turn right on the access road. In just 15 meters, turn right on an unmarked old gravel road. This converges quickly with North Shore Road, just across from your car.

There are many other hiking opportunities at Promised Land, ranging from the 1.5 km Conservation Trail to all-day hikes in the Bruce Lake Natural Area to the north (see Hike 40) to an extensive system of trails west of PA 390. Promised Land has 50 km of trails. If you are looking for trails, not farmland, this truly is a Promised Land in the Poconos.

43

Thunder Swamp Trail

Location: on PA 402 north of Stroudsburg

Distance: 15.1 km (9.4 miles)

Time: 5¼ hours

Vertical rise: 250 meters (820 feet)

Highlights: cascades

Maps: USGS 7½' Twelvemile Pond; Thunder Swamp Trail System map

The Thunder Swamp Trail in Delaware State Forest is one of the gems of the Poconos. Actually, there is no Thunder Swamp; the Youth Conservation Corps crew that opened the trail back in the 1970s liked the name. The trail system itself has a main loop centered on PA 402, along with additional side trails and loops.

The Pocono plateau was heavily glaciated, so it contains many natural lakes, ponds, bogs, rapids, and waterfalls; other lakes have been created by dams. Glaciation scrambles the drainage patterns of a region.

The Delaware State Forest consists of 29,000 hectares in Pike, Monroe, and Carbon Counties. There are many housing developments in Pike County. These are first, not second, homes, in many cases, because Times Square is only 90 minutes away. The Thunder Swamp Trail is one of the features that people fled the city to find.

You will want your boots for this rocky trail, which has streams to cross and many wet spots.

How to Get There
This is a car-shuttle hike. To drop off your first car, take exit 8 off I-84. Drive south on PA 402 for 10.9 miles to the Burnt Mills parking area on the east side of the road. Leave one car here. Then continue south for 6.1 miles to Thunder Swamp trailhead parking, also on the east side of PA 402.

To reach the Thunder Swamp Trail from I-80, drive north on US 209 to Marshalls Creek, then take PA 402 north.

The Trail
Head into the woods, following blue paint blazes, from the north end of the parking area. Immediately the trail enters from west of PA 402 and you pass a trail register. The trail continues through an open forest of oaks

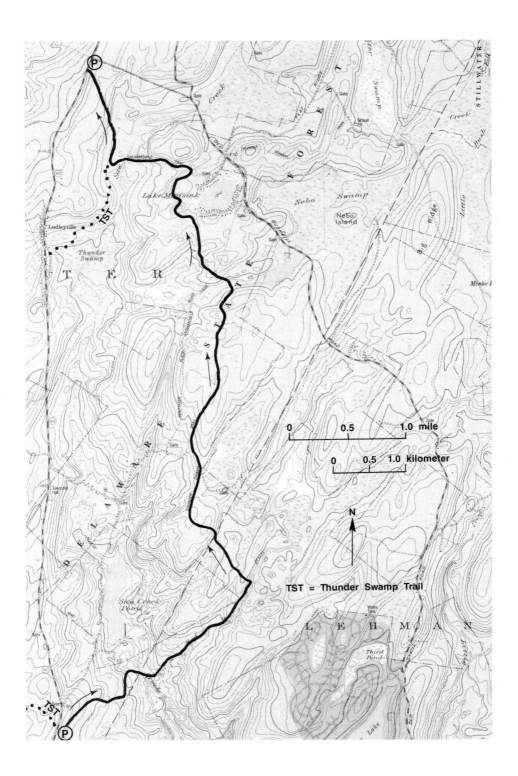

TST = Thunder Swamp Trail

and maples; farther on, you cross a stream on rocks. At 1.3 km, turn left at a junction with a trail that used to be red-blazed and that returns to PA 402.

Cross the stream again and continue to Saw Creek. There is a junction with a red-blazed trail at 2.1 km. At 2.2 km, cross Saw Creek on a footbridge built by Keystone Trails Association volunteers back in October 1986.

Now move upstream along Red Rock Run. There are many small cascades, then a large one at 2.5 km. Cross a power-line swath and continue upstream.

At 4.5 km, turn left on a woods road and leave the run behind. Shagbark hickory grows here, as does highbush blueberry. Next, turn right at a junction of woods roads and climb. Bear right where the roads come together and walk among some pitch pines. Note old orange blazes on some trees. (The Thunder Swamp Trail was originally blazed orange, not blue.)

This route passes stands of witch hazel, a shrub that blooms in the fall. The yellow flowers look like those of forsythia, only there generally aren't as many. Witch hazel may continue to flower until the snow flies.

Bear left on Red Rock Run Road at 6.6 km, pass a log landing to the right, and turn right on a trail. It climbs a low ridge and at 8.7 km crosses an intermittent stream. Then it crosses an old stone wall—no shortage of building material here. Did some optimist try to farm this land?

At 8.9 km, you come to a confusing section. Turn left on a woods road, then left again where there are no blazes (due to a shortage of large trees). The blazes soon start up again, though, and you bear right on trail. Pass a pond to your left, then through a no-cut buffer between two clear-cuts. Cross an intermittent stream, followed by Whittaker Road with its power line at 10.2 km.

Cross another stream and climb to where you can see Lake Minisink through the trees. Walk along the edge of a cliff to a junction of blue-blazed trails at 12.3 km. Turn left on a forestry road toward Saw Creek. (To your right, a blue-blazed trail leads to the Stillwater Natural Area.)

At 13.4 km, the blue blazes turn left again along Saw Creek. Continue ahead on a road bridge over Saw Creek; this route is red-blazed. Pass over a stream in a culvert and gradually climb to a vehicle gate at 15.0 km. The Burnt Mills parking lot is just beyond.

Additional hiking can be found at the nearby Big Bear Swamp (Hike 41) and Pennel Run (Hike 39) Natural Areas, as well as along other parts of the Thunder Swamp Trail System.

44

Painter Creek Loop

Location: 12 miles east of Wilkes-Barre

Distance: 15.6 km (9.7 miles)

Time: 5¼ hours

Vertical rise: 280 meters (920 feet)

Highlights: Pinchot Trail, view, mountain bogs and stream

Maps: USGS 7½' Thornhurst, Pleasant View Summit, Avoca, Moscow; Pinchot Trail map

The Lackawanna State Forest is one of Pennsylvania's smaller state forests, with only 3300 hectares divided into two tracts, one on each side of the North Branch of the Susquehanna River. This circuit hike is in the Thornhurst tract, east of Wilkes-Barre on the Pocono plateau.

The Pinchot Trail was built by the Northeast Group of the Sierra Club but is now managed and maintained by the Pennsylvania Bureau of Forestry. The trail is named for Gifford Pinchot, first chief of the US Forest Service, twice governor of Pennsylvania, and America's first professional

forester. (See Hike 4 for more information on Gifford Pinchot.)

There is a lot of good footway on the Pinchot Trail, but there are also some rocks and wet areas, so wearing your boots is advisable for this hike.

How to Get There

Despite its proximity to Wilkes-Barre, the trailhead on Bear Lake Road is difficult to find. From the east it can be reached from exit 6 off I-380. Turn north onto PA 435 at a confusing (and dangerous) junction at a red blinker. Avoid taking I-380 west. Drive north for 1.5 miles and turn left at a yellow blinker. A sign says THORNHURST 7 MILES. This is SR 2013, also known as River Road. Follow River Road for 5.9 miles, then turn right onto Pine Grove Road and drive 1.5 miles to a stop sign. Turn right onto Bear Lake Road (SR 2016) and follow it for 2.5 miles to the Pinchot trailhead.

From the west, take exit 49W off I-81. Avoid the airport and drive west on PA 315 to the second traffic light in Dupont (1.1 miles). Then turn left on Suscon Road and drive about 12 miles to the trailhead.

To reach the Pinchot Trail from I-80, take exit 43 and drive north on PA 115 toward Wilkes-Barre. It is 4.6 miles

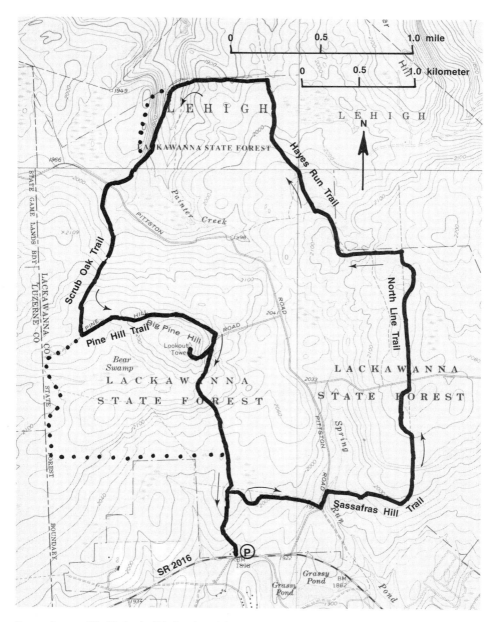

from the traffic light in Blakeslee (the junction is with PA 940) to a paved road, SR 2040 (which will change to SR 2013 at the county line). Turn right and drive 5.1 miles to a junction with Bear Lake Road (SR 2016). Turn left and drive 4.3 miles to the trailhead.

The Trail

Follow the blue blazes into the woods on stepping-stones. This is the Powder Magazine Trail. At a well-made trail register, sign in. Trail maps may be available here. Next, pass sheep laurel, mountain laurel, and highbush blueberry (ripe in July). The berry picker on the other side of the bush may be a bear. Then pass a notable shad tree; most shadbushes never get this big. Black gum and gray birch also grow along the trail.

At 700 meters, pass a junction with the red-blazed Pine Hill Trail, on which you will return. Cross a stream on rocks and note the tamarack growing in the acid soil. Jog left 120 meters on Pittston Road, then continue on the Sassafras Hill Trail. Cross a spring area and turn right briefly before resuming your easterly course. In May look for painted trilliums—and, yes, sassafras trees really do grow here.

Turn left at 2.7 km to head straight north. Next, make a brief excursion to the west, returning to your northerly course at Sassafras Road. There is a parking area to the right.

Continue on a grassy swath along the North Line Trail to a "permanent herbaceous opening," which is jargon for wildlife food. Note the fruit trees planted in plastic tubes. The tubes keep deer from eating the trees until they get big and tough. Solar ultraviolet will degrade the plastic tubes after some years.

Continue north on trail through birch trees. A path this straight must have once been a fire lane or an old boundary line. The footway is excellent. Climb a bedrock ledge and bear right past a small swamp. Turn left on the Spruce Hill Trail at 5.2 km.

At 5.5 km there is a wet meadow of wild azaleas to your left. In May they form a fuchsia expanse—though wild azalea is usually pink. The trail turns rough and rocky until 6.1 km, where you proceed on a woods road. Then turn right on a trail, which is probably Hayes Run; there is a post but no sign at this junction.

Pass pitch pines as you follow a grassy footway. At 7.7 km, turn left on the Painter Creek Trail along the state forest boundary—white blazes. Then cross a seep area (a diffuse spring, and important for wildlife survival in winter) and descend steeply. Cross an old road, then Painter Run on a log bridge. Painter Run is shaded by hemlock and spruce.

At 8.6 km, turn left on a red-blazed trail for a gentler climb. The trail soon passes an old logging railroad grade; you can see where the ties rotted in place. Ties were not treated with creosote, so they lasted only a few years and were not reused.

Rejoin the main trail at 9.4 km. Jog left around a swampy area and continue to Pittston Road at 9.7 km. Proceed on the Scrub Oak Trail and continue to climb. Toward the top, scrub oaks really do grow along the trail. The presence of this species indicates some of the poorest soil in the state.

Turn left on the red-blazed Pine Hill Trail—actually an old grassy road—at 11.4 km. Avoid another trail to the right and continue to a steel gate. Turn right on a rough trail that passes a massive ledge to the right. At 12.9 km, turn right on a gravel road and climb to Pine Hill Vista. A tower has been built here to get you above the trees and permit a 360-degree view.

To the south you can see Bear Lake, but for the most part the Poconos form a plateau. To the north you look across the Wyoming Valley to North Mountain on the horizon. Wilkes-Barre and Scranton are hidden in the Wyoming Valley. There is usually a good breeze at the top of the tower.

Head back down the road but turn right on the Pine Hill Trail. Pass through a stand of sassafras, then cross a grassy swath. The red-blazed Frank Gantz Trail comes in from the right at 14.4 km. Frank Gantz is the retired truck driver who laid out the Pinchot Trail, as well as trails at nearby Tobyhanna and Gouldsboro State Parks. He explored the forest on foot, finding old trails and grades as well as new routes and deciding just where the trail should go. The trail between the two parks is also named for him. Without such dedicated volunteers, hiking in our state would be impoverished.

Continue past a spruce plantation on the left to Powder Magazine Trail. Turn right on the blue blazes and retrace your steps to the parking lot.

More hiking opportunities in Lackawanna State Forest are found on the Pinchot Trail System; see Choke Creek Trail, Hike 36. Other loops are also possible along the blazed trails and low-use forestry roads.

45

Fourth Run

Location: Hickory Run State Park, near the junction of I-80 and PA 9

Distance: 20.0 km (12.4 miles)

Time: 6 hours

Vertical rise: 285 meters (940 feet)

Highlights: mountain streams

Maps: USGS 7½' Hickory Run; park map

This circuit hike makes a grand tour of the extensive trail system at Hickory Run State Park. Although you will only use four trails, you will intersect five others along the way.

Mountain laurel

Of course there are rocks and wet spots, some of them very wet, so you will want your hiking boots. Bicycles are prohibited on trails at Hickory Run.

How to Get There

The trailhead is a parking area on the south side of PA 534, about 0.1 mile before the park office. Hickory Run State Park is reached from exit 41 off I-80. Follow PA 534 east; this road traverses the park. See Hike 38 for more detailed directions to Hickory Run State Park.

The Trail

Start your hike by crossing PA 534 and starting up the paved road. Cross a bridge over Hickory Run and continue ahead at a road junction, passing a piped spring. Bear left on the Fourth Run Trail at 0.5 km and immediately pass the Shades of Death Trail, which diverges to the right. Cross one pole line, then a second. The trail returns to the second pole line and follows it.

At 1.0 km the Manor House Trail diverges left. Most (but not all) trail junctions along this hike are signed. At 1.2 km, bear right away from the pole line, but return to it at 1.8 km. The pole-line swath is filled with high-

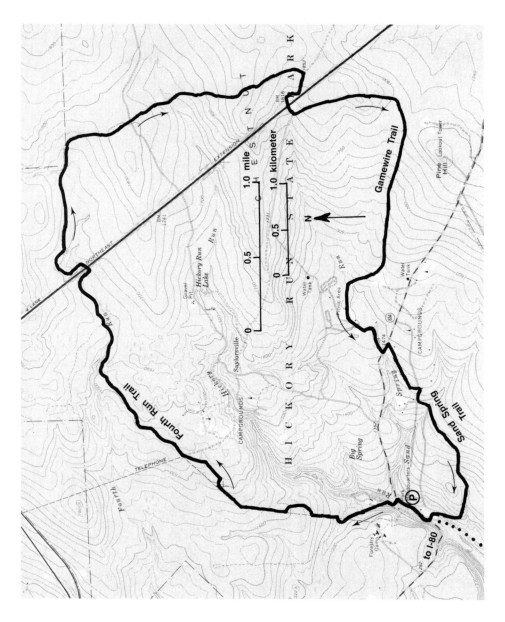

bush blueberry (ripens in July) and mountain laurel (blooms in June). Cross a stream at 2.7 km where the trail swings back into the woods.

Bear left at 3.0 km where the Stage Trail comes in from the right, leaving the pole line for good. Rhododen-dron (blooms in July), birch, and sheep laurel grow along the trail. Sheep laurel blooms at the same time as mountain laurel, but has deep pink flowers.

Cross Fourth Run on rocks at 4.7 km and proceed to a junction with the Bear Trail. Turn right on the

Fourth Run Trail and follow it to a culvert under PA 9. Here Fourth Run and the Fourth Run Trail become indistinguishable.

On the far side, the trail returns to its original alignment, which was blocked by the construction of the turnpike. At 7.2 km, cross Fourth Run for the last time and continue along the well-posted boundary of private land. Soon the trail bears right, reaching Boulder Field Road at 8.3 km.

Continue straight ahead on Boulder Field Road and cross a bridge over Hickory Run. Follow the road as it turns right at the junction with the Stage Trail and then passes under PA 9. Just beyond the underpass, turn left, then right, on the Gamewire Trail, which follows the boundary of a game reserve created by General Harry C. Trexler. After logging ended in this area, Trexler bought most of what is now the park at tax sales.

This trail has a good footway, but after a gentle descent it becomes very wet. Enter a meadow at 15.2 km, then reach a picnic area with tables, a drinking fountain, and rest rooms. There is a trail sign at this end of the Gamewire Trail. Keep right along the edge of the woods to find a pole line at the far side of the picnic area. Follow the line, then pick up a woods road that leads to a footbridge over Sand Spring Run.

On the other side bear left, passing playground equipment, to a gravel service road. Follow this road along the edge of woods, through the day-use area, past the concession stand and beach. Continue beyond the dam out to PA 534 at 17.1 km.

Turn left on PA 534 and cross the one-lane bridge over Sand Spring Run. Just after the bridge, turn right on the Beach Trail at the end of the guide rail. Ignore a trail to the right and continue past the corner of a meadow. Walk straight ahead on road at campground site 152; bear right on trail at site 158. The Beach Trail is used by campers to reach the swimming area.

At the next loop of the campground, turn left on road between sites 52 and 53. Proceed to the paved road and turn right. At 17.9 km, turn left on the Sand Spring Trail, which is marked with occasional blue diamonds. Cross a stream on rocks and bear left at a fork in the trail. The Blue Trail goes left at 18.4 km. Next, bear right along a rhododendron-banked stream to reach a trail junction at 19.7 km.

At the end of the switchback, continue ahead to the end of a paved road. Pass the park's sewage treatment plant and some service buildings. Cross a bridge over Sand Spring Run and you are back at your car.

See Hikes 28, 29, and 38 for additional hiking opportunities at Hickory Run State Park.

NORTH
MOUNTAIN

Shagbark hickory

46

Frances Slocum

Location: 10 miles northwest of Wilkes-Barre

Distance: 5.3 km (3.3 miles)

Time: 2 hours

Vertical rise: 67 meters (220 feet)

Highlights: hemlock glen, stream, meadow, lake

Maps: USGS 7½' Kingston; park map

Frances Slocum State Park, the only Pennsylvania park named for a female, honors a girl who was kidnapped by Native Americans from nearby Wilkes-Barre in 1778, when she was only 5 years old. Her first night in captivity was spent under a rock ledge—now within the park and visited on the Frances Slocum Trail. She tried to escape that night but was recaptured and grew up among the Native Americans. Mocanaquah, as they called her, was twice married to chieftains and had several children. Fifty years later, when her brothers were finally able to locate her, she refused to leave and chose to live out her life on a reservation in Indiana.

You may want your boots for this short hike, as there are many wet areas, at least in the spring. The trails at Frances Slocum were built and are maintained by volunteers from the Susquehanna Trailers Hiking Club.

How to Get There

The park is located only 10 miles from Wilkes-Barre, but it is challenging to find. From Trucksville on PA 309, turn onto Carverton Road at a sign for the park; follow signs along Carverton Road for a total of 6.8 miles, to Eighth Street. Turn left on Eighth, then left again on Mount Olivett Road. Make another left at the park's main entrance and follow this road to a T-junction. Turn right and park on the left just before the boat mooring, a distance of 1.0 mile from the entrance. This is as close as you can park to the visitors center, where the Deer Trail starts.

The Trail

Head down the closed road to the visitors center. Here you can borrow a guide to the Deer Trail. Please return it when you finish your hike. The Field Notes will explain some of the habitats and their residents you may see along the way.

Continue behind the visitors center to find the first blazes; this section

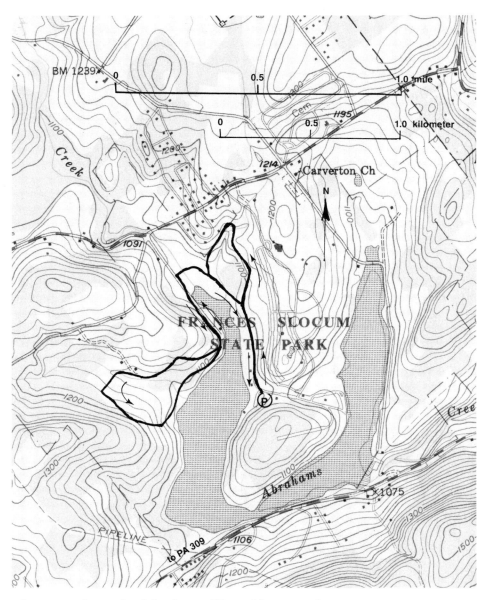

takes you along the lakeshore. The
first yellow blazes are 175 meters beyond the center. They measure 5 by
15 cm in size and are painted on trees,
posts, rocks, and even the pavement
of an old road. Variations of the Deer
Trail have a diagonal black stripe across
their blazes. If you follow one type of
blaze on the way out, you can vary
your return by following the other on
the way back.

Beware of unblazed trails along the
Deer Trail. They appear to have been
worn by mountain bikes and are not
shown on the park map.

The plain yellow blazes lead you

along a graveled path, which soon becomes dirt or mud in-season. When you enter the hemlocks, look for a black-slash-blazed trail that comes in from the right. This leads to the large parking lots in the middle of the park, but it is shown slightly wrong on the park map. Follow the yellow blazes.

The trail now enters a hemlock glen above a small stream. Descend and cross the stream on rocks, then head downstream. Bear right at the junction with a black-stripe-blazed trail entering from your left.

Next, enter a brushy meadow and bear left. At 1.2 km, cross a bridge over Abrahams Creek. Beyond the creek, turn left on an old paved road. (There is a variation of the trail to the right that circles the bay. I suspect it was used before the artificial stepping-stones were installed along the old road. It appears to be somewhat overgrown now.)

Along the road you soon reach a row of artificial stepping-stones. Take a good look at them. They consist of fire rings that have been filled with concrete, and are the most stable stepping-stones you are likely to find anywhere.

The Deer Trail is well named. You will see many tracks in the wet places and are likely to see the deer themselves. They just stand there and look back at you.

Turn right off the old road at 1.8 km, just before it enters the lake. (Really—the road predated the lake.) Keep right, then bear left at an old stone wall. The woods are filled with such walls, mute testimony to the backbreaking labor required to farm these lands.

Turn right on another old road between stone walls, then climb a rock outcrop on well-made stone steps. Turn left, then left again to reach a stream. Cross on the ruins of an old dam.

Soon the trail descends to the lakeside and heads back. Look for signs of beaver activity along this shore. Cross two streams on rocks and pass a spring. At 3.4 km, turn left on the old paved road and retrace your steps back across the bridge over Abrahams Creek. At 4.3 km, bear right following the black-striped blazes and cross a stream on rocks. Then bear right at the plain yellow blazes and return to the visitors center.

Additional hiking opportunities at Frances Slocum include the Lake Shore and Frances Slocum Trails in the main part of the park, and the Larch Tree Trail north of the campground on the far side of the lake.

47

Joe Gmiter

Location: about 6 miles west of Harveys Lake

Distance: 7.2 km (4.5 miles)

Time: 3¼ hours

Vertical rise: 320 meters (1050 feet)

Highlights: State Game Lands

Maps: USGS 7½' Noxen; Joe Gmiter Trails map

Painted trillium

The Joe Gmiter Trails are four trails in State Game Lands 57 south of Noxen and west of PA 29. The different trails are marked, in order of increasing length, with red, blue, yellow, and orange metal blazes nailed to trees. The trails are on Sorber Mountain and use many of the same sections.

They were built by the Susquehanna Trailers Hiking Club in honor of Joe Gmiter, who was president of Susquehanna Trailers for many years. State Game Lands 57 is the second largest in the state; Sorber Mountain is an isolated section of it east of Bowman Creek.

Maintenance of these trails has been turned over to a Boy Scout troop. The Game Commission permitted only *one side* of the trees to be marked. Consequently, all these loops must be hiked in a counterclockwise direction.

The Game Commission does not receive any money from general tax revenue. Its support comes from the sale of hunting licenses and other taxes on hunting supplies. Hikers do not contribute, through user fees or in any other way, to the purchase or maintenance of game lands, so permission to build hiking trails on game lands is really quite generous.

Because of this hike's steep hills and many wet spots, wear your hiking boots.

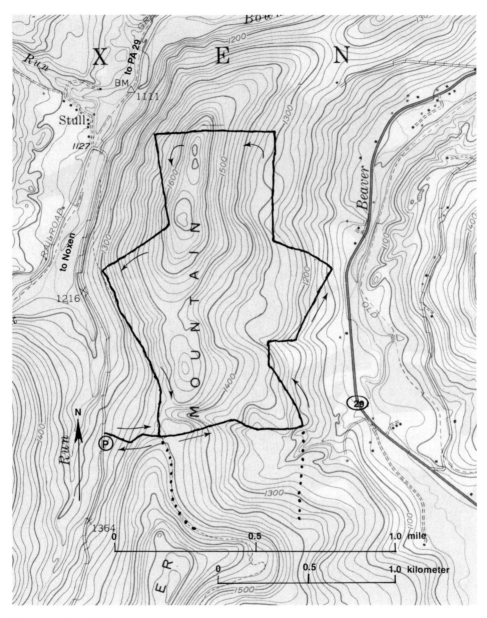

How to Get There

The Joe Gmiter trailhead can be most easily reached from PA 29 at Noxen. Turn north at the right-angle bend in PA 29. Turn left immediately beyond the bridge over Bowman Creek after just 0.2 mile. Turn left on Sorber Mountain Road in 2.3 miles and re-cross Bowman Creek. This intersection marks the location of the ghost town of Stull, which had a lumber mill. Drive south for 1.2 miles to the game lands parking lot.

The Joe Gmiter trailhead can also be reached from the Ruggles United Methodist Church on PA 29. Turn west on Sorber Mountain Road and drive for 3.0 miles to the parking lot.

The Trail

At the parking lot there is a large signboard and map showing the routes of the four different trails. They mostly follow the game lands borders, as required by the Game Commission—a prescription that makes for at least one very stiff climb. This hike follows the Yellow Trail, which turns out to be less than its advertised length.

Dodge around the gate and head up the jeep road. Where the jeep road turns right, continue ahead on a grassy road. Note the young forest to your right, resulting from a timber sale.

Reach a major trail junction at 380 meters. The Red Trail comes in from your right, the Orange and Yellow from the left. Continue ahead on the Yellow Trail. As you start down the hill, note the new growth, mostly aspen and striped maple, on both sides of the trail. At 800 meters you reach the edge of the timber sale. There appears to be heavy ATV use at this point.

Turn left at 1.0 km, leaving the ATV tracks. Here hemlocks grow along the trail. Cross a stream, noting the hobblebush growing here. The stream can still be seen to your right as you continue.

At 1.4 km you reach another junction: The Blue and Orange Trails come in from the right and the Yellow bears left along the game lands boundary. This boundary is abundantly marked with white paint blazes, and you will follow them for most of this hike. In May, look for painted trilliums here.

Continue on an old woods road to 1.7 km, where you bear left along the game lands boundary. Follow another woods road, then a logging road, crossing several small streams. Turn right to return to the game lands boundary at 2.2 km, where you turn left. Next, turn right at a boundary corner.

At 2.8 km turn left at another corner. Follow an old grade for a bit. Ground cedar and lots of ferns grow along this section. Switchback down to a stream and cross it on rocks at 3.1 km. Note the rubbish heap on adjacent private land. Would we need landfills if our public lands were privatized?

Turn left along the boundary at 3.3 km and climb. Note a red pine growing on adjacent private land. The trail turns right along a more or less level section of the boundary. Listen for the call of the pileated woodpecker: a loud *kikkik-kikkik-kik-kik*. The pileated is a bird of the deep woods.

At 4.1 km turn left and climb. Look for a white or paper birch. The climb becomes very steep near the end. Reach the viewless top, with a stand of hemlocks, at 4.5 km. Then descend to 4.8 km, where you turn left and slab up the side of Sorber Mountain. A jeep road can be seen to the right on private land. Don't take it. It diverges from the boundary, which you follow to 5.4 km.

Turn right and descend steeply. At 5.6 km, where an extra row of white blazes diverges to the right, continue ahead. Reach a trail register at 5.9 km and turn left on a jeep road that climbs gently. There is a great deal of mountain laurel here. At 6.9 km, turn right at the major trail junction and return to your car on Sorber Mountain Road.

The Red, Orange, and Blue Trails on the southern part of Sorber Mountain provide additional hiking opportunities in State Game Lands 57. Maps of the Joe Gmiter Trails can be obtained by writing to Harry West, Box 33-C, Noxen, PA 18636. Please include three first-class stamps.

48

Ricketts Glen

Location: 20 miles west of Wilkes-Barre

Distance: 10.7 km (6.7 miles)

Time: 4½ hours

Vertical rise: 315 meters (1030 feet)

Highlights: waterfalls

Maps: USGS 7½' Red Rock; park map

Ricketts Glen is the jewel in the crown of eastern Pennsylvania hiking. It is located on the Allegheny Front in Ricketts Glen State Park, between Williamsport and Wilkes-Barre.

Ricketts Glen is in the glaciated portion of the state. One result of glaciation is the destruction of original drainage patterns when preglacial valleys are blocked or filled. When the glacier recedes, streams cut new valleys. These young valleys are V-shaped and may contain waterfalls—lots of waterfalls. Marcia Bonta, author of *Outbound Journeys in Pennsylvania,* counts 33 waterfalls in Ricketts Glen; the park map identifies only 23.

Ricketts Glen is large by state-park standards; it was even proposed as a national park back in the 1930s, although World War II put an end to those plans. The park has over 5000 hectares, and adjacent game lands another 34,000. Together they constitute a significantly large tract of wild land.

The park is named for Robert Bruce Ricketts, who rose from private to colonel during the Civil War. Ricketts commanded Battery F at Gettysburg and helped repulse a Confederate attack on July 2, 1863. After the war he acquired vast holdings of virgin timber here, which could not be logged due to the absence of railroads. A railroad was finally built in 1890, and then logging started in earnest. By 1913 the virgin timber had all been cut, and the lumber town of Ricketts became a ghost town.

Curiously, the waterfalls weren't discovered until 1865. Colonel Ricketts hired a crew to build the trail past the falls. It took 28 man-years of backbreaking labor to complete the trails by 1893. As you will see, these trails require constant maintenance today. Large trees fall across them, steps are carried away by slippage, and bridges are swept away by floods.

Wear good hiking boots for this trip.

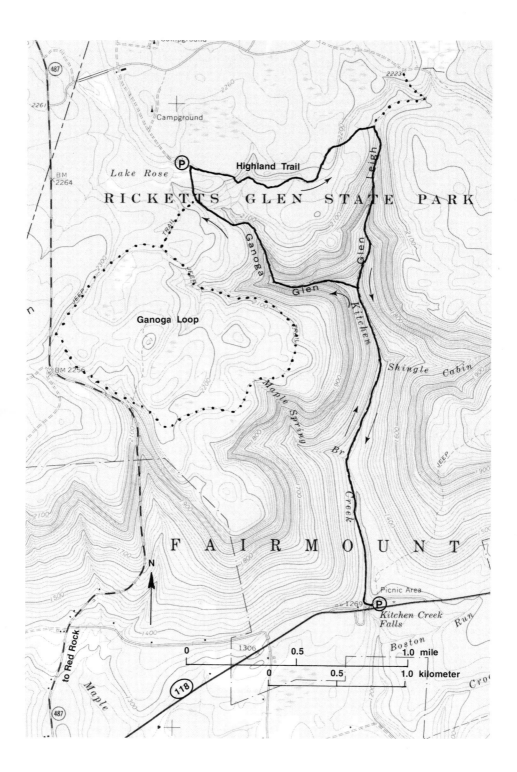

Ricketts Glen

You will need their traction around the falls. As the trail climbs each falls it is forced into the side of the canyon wall, where seep springs and spray from the falls keep the rocks wet and the mud liquid. This hike is not advisable for small children, and should be avoided if there is any ice present.

How to Get There
The trailhead for this hike is on PA 118, just 1.6 miles east of its junction with PA 487 in Red Rock. There is a large parking lot on the north side of the highway, just east of the bridge over Kitchen Creek.

The Trail
Head west and find a footbridge over the creek. On the far side, turn right and head upstream. Soon you begin to pass large hemlocks. The timber here was never cut and these trees are centuries old. Cross a bridge over the creek. At 1.3 km, return to the west side of Kitchen Creek and continue upstream. Then turn left and climb to a higher grade for a better footway. The two trails are reunited at Murray Reynolds Falls. After this, the falls come thick and fast, beginning with Sheldon Reynolds and Harrison Wright.

Reach Watersmeet at 2.7 km. Here Glen Leigh and Ganoga Glen unite. Continue up Ganoga Glen (you will return down Glen Leigh). The next falls is Erie, followed by Tuscarora, Conestoga, and Mohican. Many of the falls are identified with signs—but you may have to look around to find the signs.

The waterfalls are in an enchanted setting with brilliant green moss, multilayered shale, and huge hemlocks leaning over; the smaller falls are as beautiful as the larger, and each unique; some are single cascades, others have two or three different cascades, one above the other.

Delaware is a good-sized falls,

followed by the smaller Seneca Falls. This brings you to Ganoga Falls, which, at 28 meters, is the highest in the park. The trail has to switch back and forth to climb to the top of Ganoga. Note the guard cables at the top. Cayuga and Oneida are of modest size, and are followed by Mohawk.

A shrub growing in the glens is hobblebush, or witch hobble. It blooms in May. Elsewhere in Pennsylvania it has been eaten by the abundant deer herd. It would appear that deer don't frequent these glens, so hobblebush can survive.

At 4.4 km, cross a bridge and continue climbing to the Highland Trail, which connects the two glens. Turn right and follow the Highland Trail across a stream. Go through Midway Crevasse at 5.3 km; at 6.3 km, turn right on the Glen Leigh Trail.

Cross a bridge to the far side of Glen Leigh before Onondaga Falls. Note how the bridges are made with locally grown materials—hemlock logs. It would be very difficult to get other construction materials into these narrow valleys.

Onondaga is followed by F.L. Ricketts and Shawnee. Note the large hemlocks growing in the glen. Next comes Huron Falls. Then cross on another bridge. Ozone Falls requires switchbacks, as does R.B. Ricketts. Cross the stream again to reach B. Reynolds, and cross for the last time above Wyandot Falls. Then cross a bridge over Ganoga Glen at Watersmeet. Turn left and retrace your steps to your car.

If you haven't seen enough waterfalls for one day, Adams Falls is just downstream from the PA 118 bridge and can be reached via the Evergreen Trail on the west side of Kitchen Creek.

A shorter version of this hike—only 5.8 km—visits most of the waterfalls. Park at the Rose Lake lot and walk to the junction with the Highland Trail. Then turn right and descend Ganoga Glen. Return via Glen Leigh and the Highland Trail.

There are additional hiking opportunities at Ricketts Glen State Park. If the falls are dried up or icy, try the Ganoga Loop Trail. The Cherry Run Loop (Hike 50) is a real boot-buster in the eastern reaches of the park. Avoid the Grand View Loop, however, as the fire tower is fenced off and locked up—so no view.

49

Mount Pisgah

Location: 6 miles east of Troy off US 6	
Distance: 11.0 km (6.8 miles)	
Time: 4 hours	
Vertical rise: 365 meters (1200 feet)	
Highlights: views	
Maps: USGS 7½' East Troy; park map	

Mount Pisgah is an isolated hill in Pennsylvania's northern tier. It may owe its existence to a hard-cap rock of Pennsylvanian age (300 million years old). It is named for the biblical mountain in Jordan from which Moses first saw the Promised Land. Mount Pisgah is divided between state and county parks.

During the late 19th century, Mount Pisgah was a resort featuring fresh air, views, and springwater. There was a mountaintop hotel and a 27-meter observation tower. Summer people came from Baltimore, Boston, and Chicago to stay at the hotel and view the countryside from the tower. Today, the tower is gone, but several views are still open, providing vistas of the Promised Land of Bradford County.

Despite this hike's length and a few mudholes on top of Mount Pisgah, the footway is good. Walking shoes should be fine.

How to Get There

Mount Pisgah is reached from US 6 at East Troy, West Burlington, or Burlington. From East Troy, it is 4.3 miles on State Park Road (SR 4015). From West Burlington, it is 3.2 miles on SR 3019 and SR 4015. From Burlington, follow Steam Hollow Road (T 357) to SR 3019. Turn right, then right again on SR 4015. The trailhead is the parking lot at the fishing area on Stephen Foster Lake.

The Trail

Bear right on the paved road at the parking lot exit to start your hike. Then turn left on the Mill Stream Nature Trail just before the bridge. Follow this old road through a black forest of hemlocks. There is a view of wood-duck boxes out in Mill Creek. Pass a meadow, ignoring a trail to the right. White pines and birch add to the forest composition and add the flavor of New England to this hike.

Turn right on the Pine Tree Trail

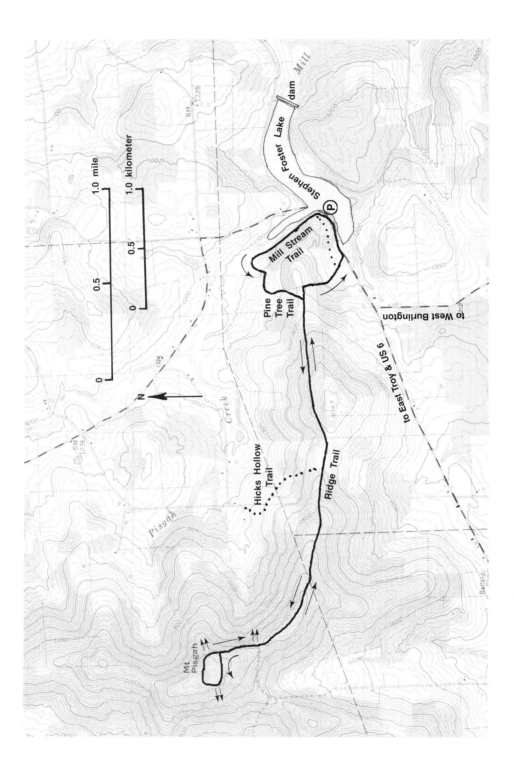

Mill Creek

at 1.0 km. Cross a stone wall and climb steeply. At the top, note an old fence made of white pine stumps. At 1.3 km, turn right on the Ridge Trail, passing hickory, maple, beech, and ash trees. Note a stone wall to the right: Serious attempts were made to farm this land. The climb continues to be steep at times.

The trail is generally 3 to 4 meters wide and provided with convenient benches. Pass a junction with the Hicks Hollow Trail at 2.6 km and enter a goldenrod meadow. There is a view of Mount Pisgah, with its microwave tower, ahead. This is a weather service transmitter broadcasting at 162.55 megahertz.

At the far edge of the meadow grow red oak and aspen trees, followed by shagbark hickory. You'll cross the unmarked boundary between the state and county parks toward the far edge of the field. Note posted private land to the left. Climb again, steeply at times. There are occasional red blazes in the county park.

At 4.4 km, reach a vehicle gate at the top of the hill. Just beyond is the end of a service road. There are a couple of picnic tables but the view to the south is overgrown with brush, scrub, and trees. Continue on the service road, ignoring a trail to the right. Instead, turn right on a paved road at 5.0 km. Remember this junction: You'll need to find it on the way back.

Immediately beyond this junction is a view to the east over rolling fields and patches of woods. Note the low cliffs at the edge. Could this be the cap rock that has preserved Mount Pisgah from erosion? Continue up the paved road and turn left on a dirt road in a patch of red pines. This road leads to the west side of the summit, but there is no view. Ignore a trail to the left, which is badly overgrown; it may once have led north to Balanced Rock.

Follow the dirt road to a children's play area and turn left, up a rise, to a pavilion on the right and a view to the west on the left. Was this where Chief Wetohah of the Oneidas meditated? His spirit is said to still inhabit this mountain.

A loop road encircles the microwave tower. Follow it down to another view to the north and east. A woods road here invites further exploration to the north. Continue down the paved road, passing another view to the north, then turn left on the service road.

Retrace your steps down the ridge to the junction with the Pine Tree Trail. This time, follow the Ridge Trail ahead. Keep right at a junction with the Marsh Hawk Trail to reach SR 4015. Cross the road and bear left on the Oh! Susanna Trail. (What else could a trail around Stephen Foster Lake be called?) Keep outside the guide rail, and soon you're back at the parking lot.

There are additional hiking opportunities at Mount Pisgah on the Oh! Susanna, Hutchinson, Marsh Hawk, Steam Hollow, Goshawk, and Haymaker Trails.

50

Cherry Run

Location: 20 miles west of Wilkes-Barre

Distance: 21.5 km (13.3 miles)

Time: 7¼ hours

Vertical rise: 225 meters (735 feet)

Highlights: deep woods, mountain streams

Maps: USGS 7½' Red Rock, Sweet Valley; park map

This is a long circuit hike in the eastern expanses of Ricketts Glen State Park—a large park on the Allegheny Front. For more on its history, see Hike 48.

The hike follows old roads and logging railroad grades of the Trexler and Turrell Lumber Company and the Albert Lewis Lumber Company, as well as a gated Game Commission road. You will definitely want your boots for this long hike, with its rocks and wet spots.

How to Get There
The trailhead is the parking area at the end of the Ricketts Glen park road; it is 1.4 miles from the park's Lake Jean entrance on PA 487.

The Trail
Head back out the park road, but take the first left. It leads past the family cabins. Where this road turns left, continue straight ahead; then, where the Glen Leigh Trail bears right, bear left. You will reach a major trail junction at 1.1 km below the Lake Leigh Dam. Note the large hole blown in this dam. Built in 1907 for hydroelectric power, it was never used. It sprang a leak in 1956 and was destroyed in 1957. Lake Leigh was named for one of Colonel R.B. Ricketts's daughters.

To the right at this trail junction is the Mountain Springs Trail—on which you will return. For now, continue ahead on the Cherry Run Trail. Note that you are following a snowmobile trail, which is marked with orange diamond markers nailed to trees. Some of the markers have lost all their paint and are now just bare metal. Pennsylvania snowmobilers pay user fees in the form of licenses and have trails built for them by the state.

The trail follows a variety of old grades, crossing a stream at 1.6 km. Turn left on a logging railroad grade at 3.5 km. This one must have belonged

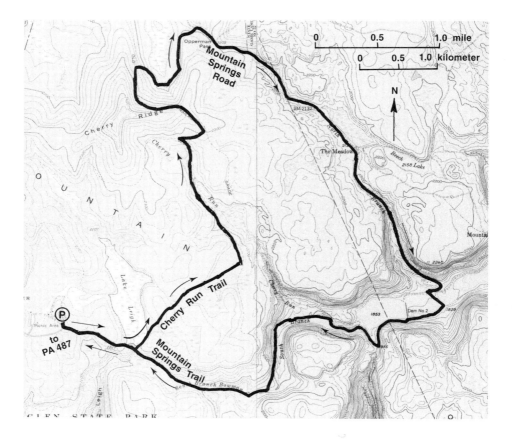

to Trexler and Turrell; it led to their mill in the ghost town of Ricketts. It's easy to follow in comparison with the ones you hiked earlier. Cross a bridge and pass a spring to your left. Cross another stream on a bridge, then cross Cherry Run itself at 4.3 km—a particularly lovely spot.

Cross a third bridge and pass a marsh to the right. At 5.1 km, there is a spring to your right set about with old iron stove parts. Presumably this was a logging camp. Next comes a large pond to the right, then a vernal pond on both sides of the trail. At 6.1 km you reach a confusing junction. A snowmobile trail marked with white blazes goes off to the right. Ignore it, continuing ahead on the Cherry Run Trail.

At 7.2 km, turn sharply to the right. This is probably not a switchback, as shown on the park map, but a siding. The railroad grade continues to 7.9 km, where you turn left on another grade that is fairly easy to follow. About 200 meters short of Mountain Springs Road, this grade evaporates and you must watch carefully for markers.

Turn right on Mountain Springs Road at 8.7 km. Efforts to break up this hike into shorter sections by means of a car shuttle are frustrated by the extreme obscurity of this junction. (Also, the Game Commission can gate off Mountain Springs Road.) This road follows an old railroad grade of the Lehigh Valley Railroad among the ghost towns of Ricketts, Mountain

Springs, and Stull.

As you walk along the road, you will pass a gated side road to the left and then the white-blazed boundary of State Game Lands 57. The stream flowing to the right of the road is the headwaters of the North Branch of Bowmans Creek. Cross a bridge and the creek expands into open water (called the Meadows) on your left. Note the many wood-duck boxes.

After you cross the North Branch again, the stream enters a gorge on the right. Keep right at 13.4 km, passing a borrow pit to the right. Continue past a closed side road at the bottom of the hill, then walk by a gate and cross a third bridge over the North Branch.

Turn left on the next old road after the bridge. (This trailhead is not quite so obscure, due to the proximity of the gate and bridge.) Then cross the South Branch of Bowmans Creek on rocks at an old railroad bridge. This spur served the icehouse at Mountain Springs Lake no. 2. A crew of 150 men was required to harvest ice during the winter, but only a small crew for shipping during the rest of the year. The foundations of the icehouse can be seen near the dam. There was another dam, also used for ice production, farther downstream near what is now the ghost town of Mountain Springs. The railroad pulled out in 1948 and put an end to the ice business.

Turn right on a railroad grade and follow it to the corner of the Mountain Springs Dam. The grade must have been altered when the dam was rebuilt and enlarged in 1964. Continue up the railroad grade of the Albert Lewis Lumber Company as it climbs above the lake and reaches a gate at the boundary of state park land. Turn right on an old road grade and follow it back to lake level. There is a good view back across the lake.

A snowmobile trail starts at the west end of Mountain Springs Lake. It is marked with diamonds, some of them still orange. Bear left on this trail at 16.1 km and follow it up the South Branch of Bowmans Creek.

You reach a confusing junction at 17.1 km; markers lead both ahead and across the creek on a bridge. These different versions of the trail probably get back together at the next bridge, but just to be sure, cross the bridge and continue up the far side. Note the old railroad ties that are visible in the short length of railroad grade just before the bridge.

At 17.8 km, turn right and climb to a more recent grade. Turn right again at a junction of snowmobile trails at 18.1 km. Bridge 2 is just to the left, and the two versions of the trail rejoin here. Bridge 3 is reached at 19.3 km. Just beyond, the Old Bulldozer Road Trail comes in from the left.

After crossing still another bridge, the trail becomes a nice grassy grade. You close the loop at 20.4 km, at the junction with the Cherry Run Trail at the foot of the Lake Leigh Dam. Turn left and retrace your steps to the beach parking area.

There is additional hiking at Ricketts Glen State Park both in the glens (Hike 48) and on the Ganoga Loop. Avoid the Grand View Loop, as the fire tower is fenced off and there is no view.

Index

Let Backcountry Guides Take You There

Our experienced backcountry authors will lead you to the finest trails, parks, and back roads in the following areas:

50 Hikes series

50 Hikes in the Maine Mountains
50 Hikes in Southern and Coastal
    Maine
50 Hikes in Vermont
50 Hikes in the White Mountains
50 More Hikes in New Hampshire
50 Hikes in Connecticut
50 Hikes in Massachusetts
50 Hikes in the Hudson Valley
50 Hikes in the Adirondacks
50 Hikes in Central New York

50 Hikes in Western New York
50 Hikes in New Jersey
50 Hikes in Eastern Pennsylvania
50 Hikes in Central Pennsylvania
50 Hikes in Western Pennsylvania
50 Hikes in the Mountains of North
    Carolina
50 Hikes in Northern Virginia
50 Hikes in Ohio
50 Hikes in Lower Michigan
Hiking Trails of Nova Scotia

Walks and Rambles series

Walks and Rambles on Cape Cod
    and the Islands
Walks and Rambles in Rhode Island
More Walks and Rambles in Rhode
    Island
Walks and Rambles on the
    Delmarva Peninsula

Walks and Rambles in Southwestern
    Ohio
Walks and Rambles in Ohio's
    Western Reserve
Walks and Rambles in the Western
    Hudson Valley
Walks and Rambles on Long Island

25 Bicycle Tours series

25 Bicycle Tours in Maine
25 Bicycle Tours in New Hampshire
25 Bicycle Tours in Vermont
25 Mountain Bike Tours in
    Vermont
25 Bicycle Tours on Cape Cod and
    the Islands
25 Mountain Bike Tours in Massa-
    chusetts
25 Bicycle Tours in New Jersey
25 Bicycle Tours in the Adirondacks
25 Bicycle Tours in the Hudson
    Valley
30 Bicycle Tours in Wisconsin

25 Mountain Bike Tours in the
    Hudson Valley
25 Bicycle Tours in Ohio's Western
    Reserve
25 Bicycle Tours in Eastern
    Pennsylvania
25 Bicycle Tours in Maryland
25 Bicycle Tours on Delmarva
25 Bicycle Tours in and Around
    Washington, D.C.
25 Bicycle Tours in Coastal Geor
    and the Carolina Low Cor
25 Bicycle Tours in the T
    Country and West

We offer many more books on hiking, fly-fishing, travel, nc
Our books are available at bookstores and outdoor su
For more information or a free catalog, please call 1-800-245-
The Countryman Press, PO Box 748, Woodstock, Verm
You can find us on the Internet at www.wwnorton.